THE GODOLPHIN ARABIAN
From an old print

# ARAB HORSES
## and
# THE CRABBET STUD

by

Spencer Borden

Caballus Publishers

**SPECIAL EDITION**

This is a special edition, limited to 1500 copies, arranged in such a manner that Spencer Borden's work is complimented by information about the Crabbet Stud. All rights to this special arrangement and newly added material are reserved, and may not be reproduced in any form without permission from the publisher.

From *The Arab Horse* and
*The Crabbet Arabian Stud of 1924*

Printed in the United States of America

# CONTENTS

# EDITOR'S PROLOGUE

It is evident from these writings of Spencer Borden that he held great respect for the authority of the Blunts, Mr. Wilfred Scawen Blunt and his wife Lady Anne Blunt. He sketches their travels among the Bedouins and describes the origin of many of the horses they purchased. He writes, "The Blunts have owned and bred so many pure Arabs since they became interested in them in 1877 that it would be a long list were all the animals named. In 1905 they had about a hundred and twenty-five in the Crabbet Stud, besides many others in Egypt. "Further evidence of his admiration and respect for the Blunt's breeding program is found in his quote of Lady Anne Blunt, "As it is a fundamental principle at the Crabbet Arabian Stud that no stallion, however individually excellent, is eligible for service if there is any doubt or lack of information as to a true Arabian descent, it follows that at this stud any 'not proven' element must remain an insuperable objection. "

That Spencer Borden considered a treatise on the Arab horse necessarily riddled with accounts of the Blunts and their Crabbet Stud is evidenced by his closing remarks about early Arab horses in America. "In 1906 three more mares came from Crabbet Park. . . . These three, combining the choicest strains of blood that ever left Arabia . . . Mr. Borden eventually brought to America nineteen Arabians from the Crabbet Stud."

It is fitting, therefore, that the original work by Spencer Borden "The Arab Horse" be placed together in one volume with the Crabbet Arabian Stud Catalog of 1926. Undoubtedly Spencer Borden would have included much of this material with his, had his book been published later.

Caballus Publishers has now combined these two historic works into one special edition limited to 1500 copies.

William E. Jones

1973

# PREFACE

In the present work Mr. Spencer Borden brings together a most interesting mass of information regarding the relation of the Arab horse to the life and history of the Arabians, and he has kindly asked me to preface the work by speaking more particularly of the natural history and of the antiquity of this breed.

About two years ago I began especially to study the Arabian after having devoted many years to the study of the horse in general. The anatomy, the origin, and the natural history of the Arab has naturally attracted less attention than the relation of the Arab to the origin of the thoroughbred racing horse. So I directed my attention especially to the structure of the animal as a perfect living machine, to the part it has played in the history of the world and to the domestication of horses from the earliest times.

This proves to be a far more fascinating subject than any of us suspected a few years ago. Darwin, in treating of the origin of the horse, among other animals, did not give the Arab an especially distinct rank. Other writers, such as the distinguished French anatomist Sansan, have pointed out the important differences in the structure of the Arab, but have not fully sustained the theory of its separateness. It remained for Professor William Ridgeway of Cambridge University to write what will prove to be an epoch-making book on the natural history of the Arab, since it forces the question of the entire separateness of the Arab breed, as a breed produced by nature before domestication by man, and entirely separate from the Northern horses of Europe.

This raises two great questions:

Did the Arab horses spring from wild horses entirely distinct from other wild horses and superior in structure from other wild horses?

Secondly, in what part of the world did the wild horses which gave rise to the Arabs have their natural home and breeding grounds?

On the first point, as to the entire separateness of the Arab breed as an original or natural breed from other horses, I am convinced not only by the arguments and facts brought forth by Sansan, Ridgeway, and others, but by my own observations that nature endowed the so-called Arab with many of its finest qualities, and that the Arabs have improved the breed but without greatly modifying it. The methods of horse rearing adopted among the Arabs are calculated to produce a fine and hardy race but the methods of selection chiefly of mares are not calculated to modify a race very rapidly. As soon as the English took hold of the Arab breed and began to select both mares and stallions for a specific purpose, namely, for high speed at short distances, they produced very rapid modifications, so that the modern thoroughbred is a very different creature from its Arab ancestor; in some respects superior, in others inferior.

On the second great question, in what part of the world this noble breed lived in its wild state, Ridgeway has advanced a largely original opinion, widely differing from that of Blunt and other great authorities on this subject, that the wild ancestor of the Arab did not belong in Arabia at all but had its home in Africa, especially in the ancient country of Libya, lying west of Egypt. He goes so far as to give this wild horse a distinct name, *Equus libycus*, in reference to its Libyan home.

I am strongly inclined to believe that Ridgeway is right. He certainly brings forth a great mass of evidence of every conceivable kind that the noble horse which has been raising the quality of the horse blood of Europe and western Asia from time immemorial came not out of Arabia but out of northern Africa. His view is naturally directly opposed to many of the interesting Arab traditions as to the great antiquity of the breed in Arabia proper, but Ridgeway shows that even Arab traditions may be interpreted to point to a remote African origin. Ridgeway's work forces a more careful discussion and examination of this question than has ever been made before, and will, I have no doubt, end in its solution.

On sentimental grounds it will be hard to take away the Arab from what we have always considered its original home and regard it as an importation into Arabia from Africa. This question is certainly not yet settled; but we may regard it as settled that whatever the issue the so-called Arabian is a very ancient breed, including characters which were strongly established in a natural state before domestication by man, and which, therefore, have such great antiquity that they are extremely stable in heredity and cross breeding.

The most profound of these heredity

characters are in the skeleton or bony framework.

The skeleton of "Nimr," like that of other Arabs, is distinguished by one less vertebra in the back, a point long ago observed by Sanson as characteristic of the North African horses. I also find that in the fore leg the ulna, or small bone of the fore leg, is complete, whereas in other horses it ends in a splint. There are only sixteen vertebrae in the tail, as compared with eighteen in the tail of the horses of northern Europe. Other characters are the horizontal position of the pelvis, as in most animals of great speed, the large size of the brain case, relative shortness of the skull, the slenderness of the lower jaw.

When one becomes once familiar with the fine points of the Arab he can see traces of the fine points of this breed impressed everywhere: there is no question that it has been the uplifting, ennobling quality which has been introduced in the blood of commoner horses

from a period dating back from 1600 to
2000 B. C.

To know the Arab horse is to love him.
Those who, like the author of the present
work, are endeavouring to maintain the
purity of the original breed, and to es-
tablish the value of its qualities, are
rendering a substantial, practical, and
theoretical service.

HENRY FAIRFIELD OSBORN

New York, May 16, 1906.

# INTRODUCTION

SOME years ago there came into possession of the writer, an old book. It had not very many pages, and they were yellow with age. One entire page was devoted to the title:

The Genealogy of the English Race Horse;
With the Natural History of his Progenitors from the earliest times. . . . . Collected from the best Authorities, etc., etc., etc.
By T. Hornby Morland.
London.
Printed by J. Barfield, Waldour St.
Printer to His Royal Highness the Prince of Wales.
1810.

In common with other writers who have studied the subject, the author argues convincingly that the blood of the pure Arab is the foundation upon which the English thoroughbred horse has been built by those responsible for his creation and improvement. He writes:

**1**

"Arabian horses are the most beautiful; they are larger, more muscular, and handsomer than the Barbs. The Arabs preserve with care, and for an amazing length of time, the races of their horses; they know all their alliances and genealogies.

.     .     .     .     .     .

"The Arabs, by long experience, know all the races of their own horses, as well as those of their neighbours."

Then follows a long account of the care given to secure properly selected mates in breeding their horses, the formalities observed when the horses are bred, the solicitous painstaking when the foal is born to make certain his identity, so that it can never be questioned, the methods of feeding and growth, of training and care. After setting out these matters with great detail he concludes:

"From all these facts it appears, that Arabian horses have always been, and still are, the best horses in the world; that from them, or by the mediation of the Barbs, are descended the finest horses

in Europe, in Africa, and in Asia; that
Arabia is not only the original climate
for horses, but the best suited for their
constitution, since, instead of crossing
the breed with foreign horses, the natives
anxiously preserve the purity of their own
race; that, at least if Arabia be not the
best climate for horses, the Arabs have
produced the same effect, by the scrupu-
lous and particular attention they have
paid toward ennobling their race, and
never permitting individuals to mix,
which were not most beautiful and
of finest quality; and that, by the
same attention continued for ages, they
have improved the species far beyond
what nature would have performed in the
most favourable climate."

These words, written a century ago,
may well serve as introduction in present-
ing the subject to be considered in the
pages of this book. The sources of
Morland's information are unknown to
the present writer. That he was well
informed, will, it is believed, become
apparent in what is to follow.

Professor Osborn, in his Preface, calls

attention to certain questions as worthy
of our consideration. First: Are Arab
horses so different from all others that
they are a class by themselves, distinct
and separate? Secondly: In what part
of the world did they first appear?

The latter question is one for scientists
to settle; it is a subject for academic
discussion alone. Before we are through
with the matters to be presented, there
will probably be few who will doubt
where Arab horses live at present and
have been found for hundreds of years in
a state of pure breeding. With this
view Professor Osborn is entirely in accord, for he writes:

"There is no question that it (the
Arab horse) has been the uplifting, ennobling quality which has been introduced
in the blood of common horses from a
period dating back from 1600 to 2000
B. C."

His statement not only coincides with
writings which will be quoted of those
who have studied the subject in Arabia

within our own times, it is confirmed
by the discoveries of Layard in his exca-
vations of Nineveh, capital of the ancient
Assyrian Empire, on the border land of
Arabia itself.  He found bas-reliefs repre-
senting men armed with spears, mounted
on horses of typical Arab conformation
and size, hunting lions.   It is a curious
fact that no horse but an Arab has ever
been found endowed with the courage to
face a lion, but that in our own day Arab
horses are frequently used in hunting the
king of beasts.

The point of most vital interest to the
present discussion is Professor Osborn's
affirmative answer to his own first question.  He expresses no doubt when he
declares "the entire separateness of the
Arab breed, produced by nature before
domestication by man. "

In this he is in entire accord with those
other eminent authorities, Sansan, the
Frenchman, and Ridgeway, the English
scientist.  Incidentally, it is of interest
that the scientific data from which Pro-

fessor Osborn partially draws his conclusions, were gathered by study of the
skeleton of the great Arab horse Nimr,
whose picture, with that of his beautiful
son Segario, we are able to produce in
these pages; a horse for several years in
possession of, and ridden by, the writer of
these lines.

NIMR

# THE ARAB HORSE

# CHAPTER I

## ARAB HORSES OUTSIDE OF ARABIA

FOR many years in Russia, Hungary, France, Germany and other countries on the continent of Europe, Arabian horses have been valued at their true worth, and studs devoted to their production have been maintained at public expense.

Peter the Great established the Imperial Russian Stud, and with his successors sought at all times to strengthen it by new infusions of pure Arab blood. Captain Ismailoff, who was sent by the Russian Government with horses to be shown at the Columbian Exposition at Chicago in 1893, tells us that as early as 1772 Catherine the Great had in the Imperial Stud, under care of Count Orloff-Tchestmensky, twelve pure Arab stallions, and ten Arab mares.

In our day the Hungarian Government
contributes annually $50,000 as added
money to the Budapest race meetings,
and $10,000 additional to meetings in the
provinces, for the purpose of encouraging
the breeding of superior horses. Not
only so, the Government maintains not
less than four great breeding studs at the
public expense, under direction of Prince
Louis Esterhazy. Of these, one at Babolna is devoted exclusively to pure bred
and half bred Arabs, and much Arab
blood is also found in the other three.
Babolna was made a separate stud, an
offshoot from Mezohegyes in 1789; and
at Mezohegyes in 1810 there were 13,386
animals, supplying at that time a thous-
sand cavalry remounts annually to the
army.

The influence of these studs of Arab
horses was forcibly illustrated in 1892,
at the time of the famous long distance
race of cavalry officers between Berlin
and Vienna. The Prussians starting at
Berlin rode to Vienna, the Austrians

started at Vienna, and rode to Berlin.
The winner of the race was Maresa, a
brown gelding owned and ridden by an
Austrian. He was a small Magyar horse,
bred in a private stud on the Stukweissen-
berge Comitat, his sire a *Gidran*, his dam
an undersized *Hotsul* or *Hocul* mare.
The mare had been given by her breeder
to one of the *czikos* or mounted stockmen,
who herd the mobs of mares that graze
on the mountains. One night a burglary
took place some ten German miles (fifty
English miles) from the stud to which
this horse herd was attached. Witnesses
swore they had seen him in the act of
robbing; but other reputable witnesses,
a number of them, were able to verify
the fact that the man was seen at his
post at eight in the evening and four in
the morning of the night of the burglary,
the alibi was decided to have been
established, and the man was acquitted
of the charge. Shortly afterward the
fellow became seriously ill and thought
himself about to die. He then confessed

that he was indeed the robber; and told
that he had ridden his mare the fifty
miles over the mountains and fifty miles
return in seven hours, besides having
committed the crime.

These Hotsuls are nearly the only
known tribe of riding mountaineers.
Their little horses are noted for great
weight-carrying power, are active, wiry,
sure-footed, untiring, and very gentle.
They are descended from the high caste
Arab horses brought into the Carpathians
by the Turks, who have invaded the
country no less than ninety times within
five hundred years. They are generally
black, bay or black-brown, and from
13 hands 2 inches to 14.2 high. They
are said to be the best shooting ponies
in the world, and can endure great hard-
ships, never tasting grain, and are pas-
ured on mountains where there is said to
be no day without rain. Bred in the
neighbouring stud of Radautz, or at that
of Mezohegyes, the Gidran—more properly Jedran, one of the highest caste

of Arab families—is either of pure desert
blood, or an Arab crossed on select English thoroughbred mares. Those bred
at Radautz range in freedom over the
wild Carpathian plateaux during the
summer, and one of these was the sire,
the little robber Hotsul mare the dam, of
Maresa, who carried his rider from Vienna
to Berlin, four hundred and twenty-five
miles, between Monday morning and the
following Thursday noon.

Not only so, but the Prussian officer to
whom was awarded the gold medal for
having the horse which should finish the
journey in the best condition, Lieut. W.
von Gaffein, was mounted on a horse of
similar breeding, a brown gelding fifteen
hands high, bred by Count Potocki in
Galicia. Though Maresa made the journey in two or three hours less time, Von
Gaffein's horse came through apparently
uninjured by the cruel test, whose severity
can be judged by the fact that of one
hundred and seventeen Prussian officers
to start, only seventy-one reached their

goal, the horses of the other forty-six
dying en route.

There is then some slight compensation
for the afflicted countries of the Balkan
peninsula, so often the scene of Turkish
rapine, in the fact that when driven out
the Turks left good horses behind them.
Constantinople was captured by Mohammed II. in 1453. His successors
Bajazet II. and Selim I. conquered Mesopotamia, and overran Syria, Palestine
and Egypt. Selim also won a great
victory over the sheik of Mecca, Lord of
Nejd, so putting him in possession of
some of the finest horses in the world.
In 1522 the Turks invaded Hungary,
500,000 strong, including in the army
their terrible cavalry squadrons number-
ing 300,000 horsemen. Having twice
besieged Vienna, the wave of Mohammedan conquest was finally rolled back on
itself by the great victory won under
Jan Sobeiski, King of Poland. It is told
that when Mustapha was finally repulsed
from Vienna, the Turkish Vizier lost his

own war horse, and that when finally
driven from the country he left behind
him "horses of rare value."

From that day to the present time the
great nobles of Hungary demand the best
of Arabian blood in their stables; and
even now a Bedouin is attached to the
Hungarian Army as master of horse,
having the rank of major, charged with
the duty of selecting the best of Arabian
horses for the royal studs. Since these
were established, in 1785, the animals
have been chosen for their symmetry,
power and action. A careful record of
their pedigrees has been kept and the
breeding carried on by a scheme of intelligent selection. Outside the government breeding establishments there are
to-day no less than one hundred and
fifty private studs, in which are to be
found 5,000 Arab mares of purest blood.

In Germany and France, also, important studs of Arabian horses are
maintained at the public expense. Some
of the animals from the stud of the King

of Wurtemburg were brought to the
United States, and are owned by Mr.
Heyl of Milwaukee, who showed them
at the Columbian Exposition at Chicago
in 1893. The French have extensive
heras of Arab horses both in France and
in Algeria. In the days of Napoleon III.
whole regiments of chasseurs mounted on
Arab horses could be seen at the great
French army manœuvres.

The greater number of Arabs imported
to America in late years having come
from England, the history of the Arabian
horse in Great Britain seems to call for
somewhat extended consideration.

John Lawrence, whose "History and
Delineation of the Horse" was published
in 1809 is one of the earliest writers on
this subject. From him we learn that
James I., Charles I., Oliver Cromwell,
Charles II. and James II. were all interested in horse breeding, and all looked to
the pure Arab horse as the source of im-
proving blood. The list of horses and
mares brought by them to England from

the East is a long one, the "Royal Mares"
being at the foundation of the English
thoroughbred horse of to-day. It was
in the reign of Queen Anne, however,
that the famous Darley Arabian was sent
from Aleppo by Mr. Darley's brother a
merchant of that city, procured by him
near Palmyra from the wandering Bedouins. Within twenty years the papers
have been found which came with this
famous horse, confirming the independent
information obtained by H. M. Consul
General at Aleppo, concerning the family
to which the horse belonged.

The Byerly Turk was brought to England some years before the Darley Arabian, and the Godolphin Arabian came
a few years after him, in 1726. These
three horses of Eastern origin have always
been considered the blood that produced
the modern English race horse, the
Arabians being the more prized. John
Lawrence wrote in 1809:

"But the fame of these two great
Arabians, the Darley and Godolphin,

has almost swallowed up that of the rest; and our best horses, for nearly a century past have been either deeply imbued with their blood, or entirely derived from it."

Time has made the truth of this assertion even more impressive. Not only so, but the process of elimination has gone on till the Darley Arabian blood has become paramount even over that of the Godolphin, several of whose sons and grandsons came to America in the early days, and were highly prized in South Carolina.

Touchstone in his great book, published by subscription in 1890, whose preface was written by the Duke of Beaufort, remarks (page 13):

"It is certain that when a thoroughbred is taken out of training early, when he is no longer subjected to that special regime which changes his outward form and modifies his constitution, he reverts to the Arab type with astonishing rapidity."

And again:

"Among the Eastern stallions which
are the originators of the thoroughbred of the present day, the eldest is the
Arab horse purchased by Mr. Darley,
a commission agent at Aleppo, and a
thorough paced sportsman, to whose
influence and energy is due in large
measure the reaction which took place
in England at the beginning of the eight-
teenth century in favour of animals of
Eastern origin.  In the course of a hunting excursion in the neighbourhood of
Aleppo, Mr. Darley met an Arab, who
was riding a very remarkable horse,
whose speed, endurance and lightness
gave him the appearance of being a
faultless animal.

"In exchange for an English musket,
a weapon very little known in the East,
and a good round sum of money, Manicka,
as this superb animal was called, became
the property of Mr. Darley, who sent
him to his brother, Mr. John Brewster
Darley, of Aldby Park, York, where he
arrived in the beginning of 1712 (1705 ?
S.-B.), he being at that time four years
old. . . . His two best representatives,
Flying Childers and Bartlett Childers,
bred by Mr. Charles Childers of Carr

House, were purchased by the Duke of
Devonshire and Mr. Bartlett.

"There is no authentic portrait of the
Darley Arabian, and we are unable therefore to reproduce him side by side with
his rival, the Godolphin Arabian.   The
important part which he played in the
formation of a pure breed must be our
excuse for this digression, and we may add
that he was a dark bay with white mark-
ings on the two near legs and a long blaze
on the head.   He was about fifteen hands
high, with a large head, well developed
haunches, plenty of length, and unex-
ceptionable limbs.   He was in fact, both
on the paternal and maternal side, of
the breed held in highest esteem by the
Arabs.

"Thanks to Mr. Darley, a fresh impulse
was given, and it was not destined to
receive any further check.   The foundation
of the Jockey Club in 1781 was the
final consecration of the work thus begun."

Major Roger Upton, with whom the
reader is to become quite well acquainted,
is most emphatic in his tribute to the
Darley Arabian. He writes ("Newmarket and Arabia," page 84):

"In itself I cannot help considering the line from the Godolphin Arab or Barb a very poor one, and, like that from the Byerly Turk, it really owes what celebrity it may have, and its continuance, to the infusions of blood it has received from the descendants of the Darley Arabian. It is worthy of remark, although not extraordinary, that almost in proportion to the amount of Darley Arabian blood has been the success of the individuals of this line."

By the end of the nineteenth century it was capable of proof by statisticians giving their attention to the subject, such as Mr. Bruce Lowe and Mr. W. A. Allison who had worked out the famous "Figure System" for the guidance of race horse breeders, that of the winners of the "Classic" English races (the Derby, Oaks, and St. Leger), since their establishment, covering a period of a hundred years, more than ninety-five per cent. were descendants in the male line from the Darley Arabian, and thoroughly saturated with his blood.

Recognition of the preponderating influence of this prepotent animal was made in a most practical manner both in England and America between 1850 and 1860, America acting first. In 1855 the New Orleans Jockey Club, at a meeting at the old Metaire Race Course, asked Mr. Keene Richards of Kentucky to go to Arabia and try to secure some of the coveted blood. About the same time, Admiral Rous of England, having conferred with other great breeders, secured the appointment of Mr. W. S. Skene as H. M. Consul General at Aleppo. He went with the definite purpose of cultivating the friendship of the Bedouin tribes, especially of the Anazah, the great breeding tribes of the desert, and of learning from them, if possible, the family of horses that produced the Darley Arabian, also if more of the same blood could be obtained. A few years later, Captain (afterward Major) Roger D. Upton, of the 7th Lancers impressed by the superiority of the Turkish cavalry in the Crimean War, because of their better mounts, urged upon the British War Office that England should procure Arab blood to freshen up the horses of the country— become tender weeds only fit to run dash races—so providing suitable remounts for the British cavalry.

Both Skene and Upton were fine Arabic scholars, besides being excellent horsemen.

For nearly twenty years Mr. Skene remained at his post, cultivating the acquaintance of the Arab Sheiks who came to trade at Aleppo, making long journeys with them into the desert, assisting them in their intercourse with the Turkish Government officials. At one time he saved the life of Suleiman ibu Mirshid, Sheik of Sheiks of all the Anazah tribes of the Bedouins, and later he interfered to save the life of another great Sheik, Jedäan. Indeed, so fast was the friendship he established with them, that they adopted him as a brother by formal rites. After eighteen years of this service Mr. Skene was able to write to Admiral Rous, that he was certain of the family of horses which produced the Darley Arabian, and his friendship with the Anazah tribes made it possible to procure a limited number of choice animals.

On receipt of the news, Admiral Rous communicated with certain English breeders, and a syndicate of three, composed of the Hon. Henry Chaplin, Minister of Agriculture, Mr. Sandeman, M. P., and Mr. Hazelwood, a director of the Bank of England, agreed to send Major Upton to Aleppo to Mr. Skene, they to go into the desert and choose and secure the horses.   It is reported that the final cost of the undertaking was £20,000 ($100,000).

# CHAPTER II

## ARABIA, AND SOME OF THE BEDOUINS

AT THE northeastern corner of the Mediterranean Sea, just below the point where the southern coast of Asia Minor joins the western coast of Syria, lies the town of Scanderoon, the ancient city of Alexandretta. This is the seaport for Aleppo, ancient Haleb, about one hundred miles to the east and a little south, for centuries a trading centre whence go caravans of merchandise to the towns far down the Euphrates, and where are brought the grains and wool that come in return. Almost due east of Scanderoon, about five hundred miles distant, is Mosul, on the River Tigris, which from this point flows south and a little easterly about four hundred miles till it joins the Euphrates near Bussorah, the two rivers thus joined

flowing into the Persian Gulf. About
two hundred miles below Mosul is
Bagdad, also on the Tigris River. The
Euphrates and Tigris nearly unite at
this point, but again separate to join
farther down, as already noted. Still
farther east, nearly parallel with the
Tigris is the western frontier of Persia.

The line from Scanderoon to Mosul
may be taken as the northern boundary
of Arabia. The western frontier of
Persia, then the Persian Gulf and the
Gulf of Oman, mark its eastern boundary.
On the south lies the Indian Ocean. On
the west are the Red Sea, Palestine, and
Syria. From this rapid sketch one can
get an idea of the great area of the country.
Coming in at the northwestern corner
from the mountains of Asia Minor, the
Euphrates River crosses the upper end of
Arabia at a slant from northwest to south-
east, and the valley of the Euphrates
has for thousands of years been a most
important route of Communication between the Orient and western nations.

Indeed, until the discovery of the way around the Cape of Good Hope, and later the construction of the Suez Canal, it was the only route and its cities were the great centres of commerce for the world.

When we speak of Arabia we are apt to forget what the country once stood for. Between the Tigris and Euphrates is the land of Mesopotamia. Here was believed to have been the Garden of Eden—whatever that may mean—the place whence the human race spread abroad to populate the earth. Mosul, already mentioned, is the site of Nineveh, capital of the great Assyrian Empire. Fifty miles south of Bagdad are the ruins of Babylon, where the children of Israel were in captivity, and within ten miles of Babylon are still to be seen the remains of the Tower of Babel. El Uz, below Bagdad, on the Euphrates, was the home of Job; and from Chaldea, east of the Euphrates, came Abraham, father of the Hebrew race.

Through this land Alexander the Great

marched to the conquest of India, after having overthrown the Babylonian Empire.  In a straight line west of Deyr on the Euphrates, and half way between that point and Damascus, is Tadmur, the ancient Palmyra, capital city of Zenobia, that Queen who was conquered by Aurelian, and carried away to Rome to grace his triumphal entry.

Later in the Christian Era Mohammed established his religion at Mecca and Medina, far down in the Arabian peninsula.  The Mohammedan Khaliphs afterward made Bagdad their capital, and held a court there that was glittering in riches, the home of art, science, poetry; the scene of the Arabian Nights Entertainments until Timour the Tartar with his hordes of barbarians poured down from the North and drowned the country in blood.  In ancient days this country was the home of science.  Some of the earliest astronomers were Arabs of Chaldea, and our present system of numerals, which makes modern mathematical calculations possible, the decimal system, was an Arabian invention, brought to the Western world by the Saracenic invasion of Palestine, upper Africa, and Europe, which was an Arabian over-running.

What is most germane to our present investigation, however, is the fact that this country is the place where the horse has attained his highest perfection; where he has been bred pure by a careful system of selection adhered to for hundreds of years, a system not departed from in the slightest degree. It has come to be acknowledged by the most intelligent breeders that thorough breeding in horses is chiefly a calculation of the amount of Arab blood they possess, just as gold stands as a measure of value in the currency of a country, the value of a coin consisting of the amount of gold it contains.

The oldest and most exclusive registry in the world—the one at the foundation of all more recent works of the kind is

"Weatherby's General Stud Book of Thoroughbred Horses," the only recognised organ of the English Jockey Club. The makers of that Stud Book recognised in the beginning, and to-day make the specific statement in writing that "Native Arabs, with the Barbs, are the source from whence the race horse springs."

The history of the Arab horse is not merely the romantic tale of imaginative writers, though poets have sung his praises, artists have painted his graceful form on canvas, and sculptors have made use of him as their model. Job describes him in words that could apply to no other horse and the horses from the frieze of the Parthenon at Athens, the Elgin Marbles now in the British Museum, could have been modelled from none but Arabians.

It is fortunate, however, that before it was too late, careful travellers, scholars and horsemen, such as Major Roger Upton and the Blunts, have visited the land of the Arab horse and written in

books what they learned from original
sources of this interesting subject.

Upton and the Blunts both made two
journeys to Arabia in the years between
1870 and 1880. In both of Upton's
journeys he had the company and assistance of H. M. Consul General at Aleppo, Mr. Skene. His wanderings were extended both in distance and in time. Hon.
Henry Chaplin, former Minister of Agriculture in Great Britain, breeder and
owner of the famous Derby winner Hermit, tells us that Upton went a thousand
miles into the desert south of Tadmur to
get the horses procured for him, and
he was gone two years. Both Chaplin
and the Weatherbys are sponsors for
the truth of every statement made by
Upton.

After Upton went Mr. Wilfrid Scawen
Blunt and his wife, Lady Anne Blunt, a
granddaughter of Lord Byron. Their
first journey was in the winter of 1877–78,
three years after Upton, and they covered
much of the same ground as he, meeting

many of the same people, though they
went also further east than Upton.
Leaving Aleppo in January, 1878, they
reached the valley of the Euphrates as
soon as possible, then followed the river
as far as Bagdad.   From Aleppo to Deyr
they had the company of Mr. Skene, who
went with Upton.   Then he turned back
to Aleppo as his consular prerogatives
went no further in that direction, the
Blunts   proceeding   to   Bagdad   alone.
From that point, after crossing the Tigris
River they went north and east to Shergat,
nearly up to Mosul, traversing a quite
new country for Western voyagers.   At
Shergat they turned west to again come
to Deyr, where Mr. Skene had agreed to
meet them on a fixed day.   This he was
unable to do.   He was old, infirm, and,
while waiting, his successor came from
England,  so  he  was  detained.   The
Blunts were most anxious to go among
the Anazah Bedouins, with whom Upton
spent the greater part of his time, and to
meet such of his friends as they might,

ARABIAN HORSES

Frontispiece of R. D. Upton's "Newmarket and Arabia"

being especially anxious to see Jedäan, their War Sheik—known as the "Rob Roy of the Desert." After great difficulties they got away from Deyr, and in due time reached Tadmur, about half way in the direct line between Deyr and Damascus. Near this point Mr. Skene overtook them, went with them among the Anazah, helped them to buy horses and continued with them to Damascus. From that point the Blunts returned to England via Beirut, Mr. Skene went back to Aleppo. The next winter found the Blunts again at Damascus, from which point they made a journey across the southern desert to Nejd, a part of the world not reached by Upton; in fact a place that no more than half a dozen Europeans are known to have ever seen.

The results of Upton's visit were written in two books, "Newmarket and Arabia," a sketchy statement of early impressions, and a more serious work, "Gleanings from the Desert of Arabia," published after his death; now, unfortunately, out of print, and copies extremely difficult to obtain.

Lady Anne Blunt also wrote two books of absorbing interest, "The Bedouin Tribes of the Euphrates," a journal of her first journey, and the "Pilgrimage to Nejd," the story of the second. No one can read these books without being impressed with the veracity and intelligence of the writers. Weatherbey & Sons, publishers of the "General Stud Book," say that they consider Mr. Wilfrid S. Blunt and Lady Anne Blunt the foremost living authorities on Arab horses. On these sources of information the present writing in large measure depends, wherever they touch the matter in hand.

Some of the individuals met by Upton and the Blunts were most interesting personages. Their introduction to the reader will help him to appreciate the sources of information, and the surroundings whence came many very great mares and stallions.

The Anazah Bedouins have always been

the greatest horse breeders.  Each tribe
of the Anazah has its individual leader or
Sheik, and at the time of Upton's visit
all the tribes of Anazah were united under
one very remarkable man named Suleiman ibn Mirshid, who was called the
Sheik of Sheiks.   He was not only a
great warrior, but also a wise adminis-
trator of the internal affairs of the tribes.

Some years before the time of Upton's
visit the Shammar tribes had been united
also under a great leader named Abd-ul-
Kerim.  The Shammar were Bedouins
who came originally from Nejd, one
thousand or fifteen hundred miles lower
down in the Arabian peninsula.  Some-
thing more than two hundred years ago,
under the guidance of a Sheik named
Faris, they had come north with their
flocks and camels, invading the pasture
lands always occupied by the Anazah.
These latter did not hesitate to wage war
on the Shammar, and drove them across
the Euphrates into Mesopotamia, to a
point near Mosul.  Abd-ul-Kerim was

the descendant of that Faris in the sixth generation, and inherited the feud that always existed between the Shammar and the Anazah, periodical raids across the river being the consequence, in both directions; the land between the Tigris and Euphrates being considered the home of the Shammar, that between the Euphrates and Damascus, and reaching from the neighbourhood of Aleppo far south toward Jebel Shammar, being the pasture lands conceded to the Anazah. The vital importance of protecting these pastures and the necessity for extensive ranges will be understood as we read from Lady Anne Blunt's first book, that she saw together in one place a hundred and fifty thousand camels, besides thousands of sheep and many horses, all the property of a single tribe of Anazah, the Roala, whose tents covered an area of 12 square miles. These great encampments had to be moved every few days because the pasturage was eaten down to the bare ground in very short order

by the thousands of animals feeding
thereon.

Yet Abd-ul-Kerim, though bound by
hereditary obligation to fight the Anazah
whenever and wherever they met, regarded
the amenites of life, and his honour became a proverb throughout the length and
breadth of the desert. It happened that
at one period of his life, in his boyhood,
he lived among the Anazah in the tents
of Jedäan's father. So, though when
they had grown to manhood these two
were bound to be always at war, Abd-
ul-Kerim never forgot his affection for
his boyhood friend. It happened then
that Abd-ul-Kerim, in the course of the
civil war, caught Jedäan's forces in such
a position that they were at his mercy.
The trap was to be sprung on the morrow
and Abd-ul-Kerim meant to push his
advantage to the utmost. Yet he wanted
to spare Jedäan individually. Therefore,
the night preceding the day of the climax,
he sent one of his men to Jedäan's camp
with his own white mare, bearing a mes-

sage to Jedäan that the morrow meant
certain defeat for the Anazah, and begging
him to accept Abd-ul-Kerim's mare, and
to ride her in the battle, as she was
swifter than any animal belonging to the
Shammar forces and could take him
safely away.  This Jedäan did and saved
himself.  Upton saw Abd-ul-Kerim's
mare in his possession when he visited
the Anazah in 1875, and describes her.

Shortly afterward Abd-ul-Kerim, who
had been successful in defeating the Turks
who sought to subdue the Shammar, was
betrayed into their hands by his secretary,
an Armenian.  They hung him from the
bridge at Mosul.

His brother Farhan, a reprobate, sub-
mitted to the Turks, accepted from them
the title of Pasha, and at the time of the
visit of the Blunts to Mesopotamia was in
receipt from them of a salary of £3,000
per annum.

The more noble of the Shammar, however, joined themselves to a younger
brother named Faris, who declared unend-

ing war on the Turks and all who held to
Turks.   He was visited by the Blunts,
adopted Mr. Blunt as his brother, by
solemn rites, and is described by Lady
Anne Blunt as a most brave, courteous
and intelligent genteman of distinguished
appearance and manners.

It is this policy of " divide and conquer"
that has marked the entire intercourse of
the Turks with the Bedouins.   So long
as Suleiman ibn Mirshid lived he kept
the Anazah tribes   solidly   combined.
Shortly after Upton's visit, however, and
a little time before that of the  Blunts,
he allowed himself to accept an invitation
from the Turkish Governor at Deyr, to
visit the town and make a treaty of commerce between his tribes and the Turks,
for exchange of products.   At a banquet
which was served to mark the close of the
agreement, poison was put in the cup of
coffee which was handed Suleiman, and
he fell back dead as soon as he had drunk
it.   Confusion followed among his tribesmen.

Then the seeds of discord were sown among the individual tribes of the Anazah. Their herds of camels, their sheep, their horses were so numerous that it required a wise hand to guide them safely, assigning pasturage to each tribe according to its requirements. The Sebäa and Gomussa tribes had always made use of the district between Homs and Hamah, above Damascus, on the western side of the desert. The next year when they came to their usual district they found their brethren, the Roala, there before them. These had been told by the wily Turk that their fellow tribesmen of the Sebäa and Gomussa were not treating them justly. They were advised to take their great flocks and herds, whose numbers have been mentioned, to the good pastures before the others could reach them, and were assured that the Turks would help them hold what they seized. In an evil hour they accepted the advice; Suleiman ibn Mirshid having been murdered was not at hand to arrange the

difficulty, so when the Blunts were among
the Anazah they found a factional war
being waged. Sotäam ibn Shäalin was
leader of the Roala against the combined
Sebäa and Gomussa. Suleiman had been
succeeded by his two cousins, Beteyan ibn
Mirshid and his brother, neither of whom
had a tithe of his administrative ability,
and as neither was able to wage the war
against the Roala, they had made Jedäan
their Akil, or War Sheik, to manage that
end of the tribal business.

From what has been said it is easy to
understand the wretched condition of
affairs among the Bedouins for the ten
years between 1874 and 1884. Let us
remember, also, that during that period
the Russo-Turkish war was carried on,
so that relief from the usual aggression of
the Turks, left the Bedouins free to fight
among themselves. It was during the
raids and counter-raids of this time
that many priceless animals changed
hands, to be run hot haste by their captors
into the towns bordering the desert for

sale to save them from recapture.  It is
certain that in the decade mentioned
more high-caste Arab horses came out of
the desert than ever before or since.  Some
of the animals thus coming into strange
hands will be mentioned specifically.

# CHAPTER III

## Early History and Families of Arab Horses

THE Bedouins of Arabia are a pastoral people who have lived for centuries from their flocks of sheep and herds of camels, and have bred their horses on well established lines from time immemorial. They have always been independent, acknowledging no rulers but their own Sheiks; jealous of interference by outsiders. Job was a Bedouin, and the place of his origin, Ur of Chaldea, was visited by the Blunts on their first journey in Arabia.

All the Bedouins are descendants of Ishmael, and they have genealogies dating from the earliest antiquity. It will be remembered that Abraham himself was a nomad, who came from Chaldea, the country east of the Euphrates

45

and Tigris, between those rivers and
the Persian boundary. Hagar, mother
of Ishmael, was Abraham's concubine.
After the birth of Isaac, Ishmael's half-
brother, she was driven into the desert
with her fourteen-year-old son by the
jealousy of Sarah, Isaac's mother. Arab
tradition supplements Bible history by
telling us that when Ishmael was sent
away with his mother he lamented his
barren heritage. He was assured, however, that there was reserved for him the
most valuable gift to men. This he sub-
sequently discovered was the horse of
the Kuhl race, which he found in Hejaz.

The two branches of descendants from
Abraham were as follows:

|  | *Abraham* |  |  |
|---|---|---|---|
|  | Isaac. | 1 | Ishmael |
|  | Jacob. | 2 | Kidai. |
|  | Judah. | 3 | Hamal. |
|  | Pharez. | 4 | Nabet. |
| (about 1635 B. O.) | Hezron. | 5 | Salaman. |
|  | Ram. | 6 | Alhamaisa. |
|  | Amminadab. | 7 | Alyasa. |
|  | Nashon. | 8 | Odad. |
|  | Salmon. | 9 | Oddo. |
|  | Boaz. | 10 | Adnan. |

| (about 1635 B. O.) Obed. | 11 | Maad. |
| [continued] Jesse. | 12 | Nazar. |
| David. | 13 | Rabiah (al Faras) |
| (B. O. 1033) Solomon. | 14 | Asad. |
| Rehoboam. | 15 | Anazah. |

Salaman, fourth in descent from Ishmael, living B. C., 1635, contemporary of Hezron, is recorded as owner of five mares of superlative value. Five hundred years later, his descendant eight generations further along, contemporary of David, was a man named Rabiah. It is recorded that although Rabiah was the third son of Nazar (perhaps the fourth) he was chosen by his father as the most suitable person to be entrusted with his very valuable breeding mares, and to continue their use properly, so they were given to him. and the words *al Faras* ("of the horses") were added to his name. Rabiah al Faras was the grandfather of Anazah; and from him spring all those Bedouin tribes that bear his name, who breed, and have bred for three thousand years, the purest and choicest Arab horses. Anazah inherited them from his grand-

father Rabiah, descended without taint
of foreign blood from five famous mares
owned by Sheik Salaman, he being fourth
in descent from Ishmael son of Abraham.
Major Upton sums the entire matter in
these words: "An *authentic* family of
horses has been preserved in Arabia for
3,500 years."

Until Upton had made the researches
that opened up the true history of the
Bedouins and their horses, it was common
report that these latter were descended
from mares that belonged to Mahomet.
It is capable of proof that Mahomet
never owned a horse until he went to
Medina. He then became possessed of
seven mares, three of which were bought
—their names and former owners are
recorded—and four others were gifts.
The race of pure bred Arab horses was
in existence three thousand years before
Mahomet was born.

Some writers have mentioned a family
of Nedjid horses, and of Kochlani, as
being the best strains of Arab blood.

Major Upton and Lady Anne Blunt have
taught the world that these are not families of horses at all. Nejd is the name of
a great district in the lower end of Arabia,
for centuries under the absolute control
of the Anazah tribes—Gomussa, Sebäa,
Raola, Welled Ali, Fedäan, etc.—though
not now in their possession. As these
tribes have none but the purest strains of
horses, animals whose blood has been
kept untainted for a known period of
3,500 years, the Nedjid horses (as Ameri-
cans would speak of Kentucky or State
of Maine horses) were highly esteemed by
those fortunate enough to possess them.
The word Kochlani is derived from
*Kuhl*, antimony. Lady Anne Blunt tells
us that Arab women apply antimony to
their eyebrows and eyelashes to increase
the brilliancy of their eyes, antimony
being black. Therefore, as all Arab
horses are supposed to have black rings
about their eyes, such are called Kochlani. Among the Anazah, Major Upton
found the words *Keheilan* and *Keheilet*

applied to the horses. Both words are recognised as derivatives from Kuhl (antimony) but Upton got another explanation of the meaning of the words as applied. He found that the entire race of pure-bred horses among the Anazah had black skins, no matter what the colour of their coats. It has come about, then, in course of time, that the Anazah have adopted the words, to express what we mean in speaking of "thoroughbreds." It is even more exclusive than our word. We speak of "thoroughbred" horses, "thoroughbred" cattle, "thoroughbred" dogs, meaning improved animals that are bred to a type, and have not varied from the type since the breed was established.

With the Bedouin *Keheilan* means but one thing, a horse (male) of pure Arab blood, and *Keheilet* a mare of pure Arab blood, whose lineage traces without break to one or more of the five mares of Salaman (*not* King Solomon, David's son), an Arab Sheik who lived B. C. 1635, fourth in descent from Ishmael, son of Abraham.

The Bedouins use two other words that indicate especial quality among their Keheilans and Keheilets. *Asil* is equivalent to *noble*, or *distinguished*; *Hudud* means *approved*. This appellation is used in connection with a Keheilan, who is so well and widely known among the tribes, that many seek his service for their mares, and his name only needs to be mentioned.

Upton also learned that all pure-bred Arabians were included in *Al Khamseh*, which means *The Five*. That is, the Anazah Bedouin refuses to recognise any animal as a Keheilan or Keheilet that cannot trace direct to one of the five mares of Sheik Salaman.

Al Khamseh he found is divided into the following great families:

1—The descendants of Keheilet Ajuz.
2—The Manakhi family, with three sub-families.
3—The Hadban family, with five sub-families.
4—The Jelfon family, with two sub-families.
5—The Homdani family, with two sub-families.

The first two families are the *creme de la creme* of all horses, the descendants of Keheilet Ajuz being still further divided as follows:

1—The Seglawi family (Seglawi-Jedran, Seglawi-Obeiri, Seglawi-al-Abd.)
2—The Abeyan family, with seven secondary families.
3—The Dalman family, with four secondary families.
4—The Abu-Arkab family, with three secondary families

The following are also believed to belong to the same great family of Keheilet Ajuz:

5—The Rishon family, with two secondary families.
6—The Radban family, with three secondary families.
7—The Twaissan family, with two secondary families.
8—The Milliah family, with three secondary families.

The history of Keheilet Ajuz comes to us surrounded by a romantic halo thrown around her by the people among whom she was born and lived. It is related that a certain Sheik was flying from an enemy, mounted on his favourite mare. Arab warriors trust themselves only to mares, they will not ride a stallion in war. The said mare was at the time far along toward parturition; indeed she became a mother when the fleeing horseman stopped for rest at noonday, the newcomer being a filly.

Being hard pressed the sheik was compelled to remount his mare and again seek safety in flight, abandoning the newborn filly to her fate. Finally reaching safety among his own people, great was the surprise of all, when, shortly after the arrival of the sheik on his faithful mare, the little filly, less than a day old, came into camp also, having followed her mother across miles of desert. She was immediately given into the care of an old woman of the tribe (*Ajuz*—an old woman), hence her name, Keheilet Ajuz, "the mare of the old woman," and grew to be the most famous of all the animals in the history of the breed. That such a mare really lived is not to be doubted, whatever credence we give to the story of her early life. Upton seems in doubt just where to place her. He says that some believe all the present families of Al Khamseh (the five) are descended from

Keheilet Ajuz, she being descended from one of the original Al Khamseh. Others believe that the line of Keheilet Ajuz, with her sub-families, and numerous single strains, is collateral with the other four Keheilets of Al Khamseh, and that all the families are not descended from Keheilet Ajuz. There seems testimony both ways.

Again some think the second family named as descended from Keheilet Ajuz, namely the Abeyan (Aba—*a cloak*—so named because they carry their tails so high that a sheyk once casting away his cloak in flight, it was caught on his mare's tail and carried along with him) with its seven sub-families, should not be considered by itself, though it is very choice (asil), but is really a part of the family of Seklawi Jedran.

The names of these last show how the sub-families come about. A man named Jedran had three mares, full sisters, of the Seklawi family. One he kept himself, so she was known as Seklawi Jedran.

Another he gave to his brother Obeiri, hence Seklawi-Obeiri. The third he gave to his slave, so Seklawi al Abd (of the slave). It is interesting to know that Seklawi al Abd proved a choicer strain than Seklawi Obeiri.

In closing his remarks on Keheilet Ajuz Upton says:

"Whether the era of Keheilet Ajuz was before or since the days of Rabiah, and if before, whether the horses inherited by Rabiah were solely from her, I cannot say. But it certainly appears to me that a special selection of horses does exist in the Anazah tribes, and their tenacity and persistency in keeping it pure and select is shown by their refusing to acknowledge or return to any strain which has departed from them into other hands."

The reader will have noticed that the Arabs always mention the mares from which their animals are descended, and so designate the families to which they belong. In this they are quite right. They speak with contempt of " the son of a horse." Such an animal is Kadish (a mongrel), his dam is lacking in his pedigree, and no number of generations of pure blood, superimposed on an impure foundation, can wash away the stain of an impure mare at the bottom of the pedigree. But a Keheilan is a different proposition; he is the son of a mare, a Keheilet, and no mare among the Anazah is allowed to be bred, excepting in the presence of witnesses, who can testify that her offspring is a Keheilan, son of a Keheilet.

This founding a family on a mare rather than a stallion is a certain guarantee against mongrelisation; and the Anazah do not recognise the possibility of a taint ever being covered by the intervention of never so many pure-bred sires. They look with contempt on even the best English thoroughbred, since there is not one of them whose family is not lacking in some of its female lines.

The English have an expression, "as thoroughbred as Eclipse." Yet Eclipse had 70% of unknown blood in his veins.

# CHAPTER IV

## How Some Arab Horses Have Been Obtained

A S ALREADY noted, the journeys and subsequent writings of the Blunts and Major Upton have done much to enlighten the world at large concerning Arab history and the breeding methods of the Bedouins. Through their agency, also, came to England many pure Arabs, indeed nearly all the pure bred mares that were acquired from the desert by reason of the civil wars in Arabia just preceding and following the Russo-Turkish conflict of the late seventies. One other channel only through which mares were obtained was the purchases and breedings of Abbas Pasha, Khedive of Egypt. He realised the value of pure Arab blood in horses, and spent money like water in getting the

best that could be had, both from the
Anazah in the upper desert, and also
from Nejd. In one instance, having
bought a mare of rare strain in Nejd,
and thinking her too old to make the
journey to the seacoast by using her own
legs, Abbas sent a bullock cart for her,
bringing her one thousand five hundred
miles on wheels.

All of these, Upton, the Blunts, and
Abbas Pasha, got stallions also, as did
Hon. Miss Ethelred Dillon and others,
while a number of valuable animals
were taken to India by the Arab horse
dealers of Bombay, Abdur Rhaman,
Eyssa bin Curtis and Eyd et Tenimi, who
sold them to British officers and Indian
Rajahs for racing purposes. We owe
the mares, however, to Upton, the Blunts,
and Abbas. When the last named was
deposed, his breeding stud was continued
for some time by Ali Pasha Sherif, and on
the breaking up of the stud the choicest
animals were purchased by the Blunts,
who, in addition to the Crabbet Park

stud in England, continue the breeding of
Arab horses at Heliopolis, near Cairo,
Egypt, under the superintendence of
Sheik Obeid, to the present day.

As descendants of many of these animals have come to America from 1888
to the present time, it will be of interest
to note some of the most valuable individuals and trace their antecedents and
subsequent history. We have already
noted that all Arab breedings are founded
on the female line, to the extent that if a
foal is offspring of a stallion and a mare
of different families, it takes the family
name of its dam, not its sire, we therefore will first consider the mares.

The first time Upton visited Arabia he
secured three animals, two mares, Zuleika
and Haidee, and the stallion Yataghan.
Zuleika produced one colt foal named
Symmetry, then died. Yataghan was
bred to Haidee and then sold to the antip-
odes. Haidee produced one foal, Naomi,
then she died also.

After the death of Major Upton, Naomi

was bought by Rev. F. F. Vidal of Need-
ham Market, Suffolk, an enthusiastic
admirer of the Arabian horse, who
owned her for several years, and bred
four foals from her. In 1888 Mr. Vidal
sold Naomi to Mr. Randolph Huntington
of Rochester, New York, who afterwards
removed to Oyster Bay, Long Island,
where Naomi died at the age of twenty-
two years.

Naomi produced the following offspring:

*In England,*  1. ch. h. Gomussa, by Kars.
            2. ch. m. Kushdil, by Kars.
            3. ch. m. Nazli, by Maidan.
            4. b. m. Naama, by El Emir.
*In America,*  5. ch. h. Anazah, by Leopard.
            6. & 7.(a mare and stallion by a trotting
               horse!)
            8. ch. h. Nejd,  by Anazah, her own son.
            9. ch. h. Khaled, by Nimr, her grand son.
           10. ch. m. Naomi II, by Nimr, her grand-
               son.
           11. ch. m. Narkeesa, by Anazah, her son.
           12. ch. m. Naressa, by Anazah, her  son.

On his second journey Upton secured
five animals whose families are recorded
pages 386, 387, and 388 of his "Glean-

ings from the Desert of Arabia." The pedigrees of the two horse colts and of one of the mares are certified under seal by Suleiman ibn Mirshid, of one mare by Jedäan ibn Mahaid, and of the other mare by both Suleiman and Jedäan.

Of these, the only mare to produce offspring was Kesia, a bay mare, a "Keheilet of Nowak," imported "in foal by a hudud Seylwi al Abd." This mare produced in 1876, in Hon. Henry Chaplain's stable at Blankney, the bay mare Kesia II.

The offspring of Kesia II. were:

1. 1887, ch. m. Nowagich, by Hadeed.
2. 1888, b. h.
3. 1889, b. h.
4. 1890, ——?
5. 1891, b. h. Imamzada, by Imam.
6. 1892, ch. m. Dabeh, by Hadeed.
7. 1893, ch. m. Mimosa, by Mameluke,
8. 1894, ch. m. Shabaka, by Mameluke,
9. 1895, ch. m.  ? by Mameluke.

Kesia II. was struck by lightning in 1898 and killed. She was the property of Hon. Miss Dillon.

The horse colts brought in 1875 by Upton were Joktam, that was sold to Australia for £1,000, a Keheilan Tamri and Ishmael that was kept by Mr. Chaplin.

Kesia had no offspring by a pure Arab horse other than Kesia II, though she produced, in 1878, a chestnut filly by the great Derby winner Hermit, as reprehensible an act in breeding as coupling Naomi with a trotting stallion.

The first visit of the Blunts to Arabia resulted in their bringing to England with them three mares—rather they were forwarded after them by Mr. Skene—Hagar, Sherifa, and a chestnut mare, Säadah Togan.

Hagar was perhaps the best mare, certainly one of the best, that ever came out of the desert. Lady Anne Blunt says of her:

" Endurance of fatigue on the road and hardiness under want of food are qualities that may always be reckoned on in buying an Arab horse, no matter what his looks or what his pedigree; but speed is exceptional, and confined to the best strains of blood.  Hagar, as we called her, was of the Keheilan Ajuz breed, the fastest, the stoutest, and the most English looking of them all.  When purchased, she was in very poor condition, having just gone through the severe training of a campaign. She was bred by the Gomussa, the most notable of the horse-breeding tribes, had passed from them to the Roala, and had now been captured and ridden some two hundred miles in hot haste for sale at Aleppo.  She was a five year old mare, a bay, with black points.  We never met anything in our travels which could compete with her over a distance, and she has often run down foxes, and even hares, without assistance; carrying thirteen stone (182 lbs.) on her back.  She was of a mild, gentle temper, and always went smoothly on, without fret or worry, and with the long low stride of an English race horse.  She never galloped better than when she seemed worn out with work.  She had the advantage, too, for Wilfrid, of being tall, fifteen hands—an unusual height among Arabians."

Lady Blunt's book, "The Bedouin Tribes of the Euphrates," is full of the praises of Hagar's performances, and one of the best was after having been ridden more than twelve hundred miles in three months of travel in the desert, from Aleppo to Deyr, Bagdad, through Mesopotamia to Shergat, then west again across the Euphrates and to Tadmar. It was when they turned back to meet Mr. Skene at Arak, after having started from Tadmar to join Jedäan in the desert.

"It was still nearly dark when we mounted, but we would not wait longer than for the rise of the morning star, and started at a gallop as soon as we had it for a guide. The Zaptiehs on their tired horses made a show of accompanying us, declaring it was impossible they should allow us to go alone. But Hagar had quite other ideas, and after the first two miles they dropped behind and were lost to sight. And now began the longest gallop I ever took in my life. It was fifteen miles to Arak, and we never drew rein till we got to the foot of the hill behind which the village stands. . . . For the first few miles my mare behaved very well, going on at her easy stride without unnecessary hurry, and allowing Tamarisk to keep more or less beside her; but after this, although she was not in the least excited, she would not be kept at any reasonable pace. She does not mind uneven ground, full of Jerboa holes, and went faster and faster, till soon Tamarisk and Wilfrid were as much out of the race as the soldiers were, and yet she would not be steadied. It was only when we came to the hills and very broken stony ground, fully twelve miles from where we started, that I got a pull at her, and at last stopped her. . . . We were just forty-five minutes doing the twelve miles. . . . The last two miles we travelled at a more sober pace, and the sun appeared as we rode in through the stone gateway of Arak."

No wonder she brought Hagar to England as a brood mare! There she produced the following:

*Offspring of Hagar.*

1. 1880, b. h. Hadramant, by Kars.
2. 1881, ch. m. Halfa, by Kars.
3. 1883, b. m. Hijaz, by Pharaoh .
4. 1884, b. m. Harik, by Kars.
5. 1885, b. m. (died) by Rataplan.
6. 1886, b. h. Himyarite, by Kars.
7. 1888, b. h. Hafiz, El Emir.
8. 1889, br. m. Zem Zem, El Emir.
9. 1891, b. h. Havileh, by Imam,
10. 1892, b. h. Hail, by Jamrood.
11. 1895, ch. h. Sohail, by Jamrood.
12. 1896, b. m. Hamada, by Imamzada.
13. 1897, b. h. Hauran, by Jezail.

Hagar died in 1898, twenty-five years of
age. The chestnut mare Saädah Togan
bought at Deyr is said to have been sold
to Miss Dillon under the name of Zenobia
but we have no record of her offspring.
Hagar also had been owned and used for
breeding purposes for a number of years
by Miss Dillon, whose property she was at
the end.

Sherifa, the white mare was a very
marked animal, " a white Hamdani Simri
purchased for us by Mr. Skene at Aleppo."
She was bred in Nejd, and was given by
Ibn Saoud, Emir of Riad, in 1873, to the

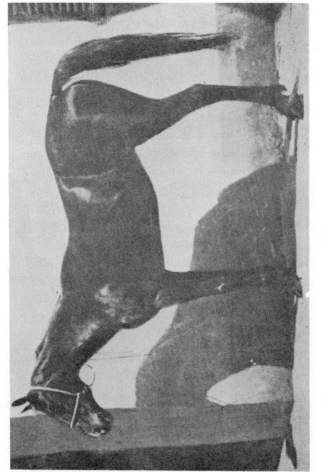

ZEM ZEM
Daughter of Hagar

Turkish governor of Mecca. He brought
her to Aleppo and gave her in turn to the
chief Ulema there, who used her only as a
brood mare and to carry him once a day
to the mosque. Lady Blunt says she had
" the most extraordinarily beautiful head
ever seen, and the sweetest of tempers."

The full list of her offspring cannot be
known, as she had foals both in Arabia
and after coming to England. In the
latter country her blood is highly prized,
not only that through her daughters,
Sherezade and Shibboleth, but also at the
present day where her grand-daughters,
Shieka and Shibine, the first a daughter of
Shiraz, the second a daughter of Shohba,
represent her in the Crabbet Arabian
Stud.

The Blunts have owned and bred so
many pure Arabs since they first became
interested in them in 1877 that it would
be a long list were all the animals named.
In 1905 they had about a hundred and
twenty-five in the Crabbet Stud, besides
many others in Egypt. A few more of

their mares, however, deserve at least passing mention.

Rodania, dam of Rose of Sharon, Rosemary, Rose of Jericho, and others. This mare, far famed among the tribes of the "Hamad," was the much prized property of Beneyeh Ibn Shäalan, of the Roala tribe of the Anazah. She was a chestnut Keheilet Ajuz of the Rodan strain, bred by Ibn Rodan of the Roala tribe. Sotäam Ibn Shäalan, supreme Sheik of the tribe when visited by the Blunts in March 1878, took her from his cousin Beneyeh by unfair means, her theft being the occasion of a feud between the two. War breaking out between the Sebäa and Roala tribes, Beneyeh refused to help Sotäam, the Roala were badly beaten, and they lost much plunder of camels and mares, including Rodania. She was taken by Tais Ibn Sharban of the Gormussa tribe of the Sebäa Anazah, from whom the Blunts bought her in 1881.

Bint Helwa, a white Seglawieh Jedranieh of the strain of Ibn Sudan of the

MARES AND FOALS AT CRABBETT PARK

Johara (sister to the " broken-legged mare ") in the centre ; Rose of Sharon to the extreme right

Roala tribe.   This is the famous "broken-
legged mare," now to be seen at Crabbet
Park.   When visiting this stud in Sep-
tember 1905, the writer had first one and
then another particularly attractive animal pointed out as the offspring of "the
broken-legged mare."   Finally he asked,
"What is the broken-legged mare, and
where is she?"   "You shall see," said
Lady Anne Blunt, leading the way to a
box stall, of which Bint Helwa was the
sole occupant.   Here we saw a broken-
legged mare sure enough.   Were it not
for her injury she is a beauty, pure white,
with a head such as Schreyer would seek
as a model.   But, her off fore leg! This
was broken between the knee and shoulder
so that it *wabbled* loosely.   Her shoulder
was also broken, and the gentle creature
stands always on three legs, the fourth
can support no weight, the toe just
touches the ground, and when she would
move about the mare rears a bit, hops
around with the good front leg, dragging
the poor useless member.

The exclamation was spontaneous, "For heaven's sake how long has that mare been in that condition?" "Oh, for eight years," answered Lady Blunt. Then she told the story. Bint Helwa had come from the Egyptian stud with two other mares, and the three turned to pasture together on arrival in England. In the evening the other two came up to the stables, Bint Helwa was missing. On searching, she was found in a ditch. She had jumped the enclosing fence of the pasture, landed in the ditch so that her leg and shoulder were terribly broken, and the other mares following had jumped on top of her, breaking two of her ribs. As she was within six weeks of foaling it was decided not to destroy her, but take her to the stable and try to save the foal. The mare was gotten out on to a drag, pulled as gently as possibly to her box stall, suspended in slings, and cooling applications made to the injured parts. The breaks were too extensive to knit, but such was the soundness of her health

and constitution that the days passed
and no rise in her temperature ensued.
When the day came for her foal to be
born, she was lowered gently in the stall,
the little one came into the world all
right, she made good recovery, *and since
that time has bred seven perfect foals.* Now
in 1906, the broken-legged mare is nineteen years old, and she is due to foal this
spring. This authentic history of a mare
that is to be seen by any visitor to Crabbet Stud is a tale of endurance and soundness that might lead us to give credence
even to the tradition associated with the
beginnings of life of the famous Keheilet
Ajuz. If there is a finer Arab stallion
in the world than Harb, the six year old
son of Bint Helwa and Mesaoud, the writer
would go a great distance to see him.

Queen of Sheba is the name of a bay
mare foaled in 1875, which Lady Anne
Blunt saw and coveted at the time she
was with the Sebäa Bedouins in March,
1878. At that time the mare belonged
to Beteyen Ibn Mirshid, who had succeed-

ed his murdered cousin Suleiman Ibn
Mirshid, Upton's friend, as supreme
Sheik of the Gomussa. She was bred
by Erheyen Ibn Alian of the Gomussa
tribe, was an Abeyeh Sherrakieh, and
was sold by her breeder, on shares, to
Beteyen. At the time of their visit the
Blunts sought by every means to buy
the filly, and the account of their efforts
as told in "The Bedouin Tribes of the
Euphrates" is highly interesting. The
mare is thus described by Lady Blunt:

"But our chief delight was to follow,
when Beteyen Ibn Mirshid, Sheyk of
the Gomussa, rode up to Mohammed
Dukhi's tent to pay a visit. He had just
purchased from one of his people the
'bridle half' of a three year old mare, an
Abeyeh Sherrak, and was riding her
home when he heard we were at Mohammed Dukhi's tent. The mare is so
much more remarkable than the man
that I must describe her first. She is a
dark bay standing fifteen hands or over.
Her head, the first point an Arab looks
to, is a good one, though I have seen

finer, but is perfectly set on, and the
*mitbakh*, or join of the head and neck,
would give distinction to any profile.
Her neck is light and well arched, the
wither high, the shoulder well sloped, and
the quarter so fine and powerful that it
is impossible she should be otherwise than
a very fast mare. Her length of limb
above the hock is remarkable, as is
that of the pastern. She carries her
tail high. as all well bred Arabians do,
and there is a neatness and finish about
every movement which reminds one of
a fawn or a gazelle. We all agreed that
she is incomparably superior to anything we have seen here or elsewhere
(Mr. Skene was of the party at the time)
and would be worth a king's ransom, if
kings were still worth ransoming."

They did not get the mare at that time,
but Mr. Skene secured her for them later
at a cost of £240 ($1,200); and when
they returned to Damascus the next
winter to make a start for their "Pilgrimage to Nejd," they heard "all that
had happened in the desert during the
summer. First of all, the sensation that

has been caused there by our purchase of Beteyen's mare, which after all we secured and the heart-burnings and jealousies raised thereby."

Asfura, daughter of Beteyen's mare, and several of her offspring are to be found at Crabbet Park to-day. Astraled, the son of Queen of Sheba* and Mesaoud, foaled 1900, is the only horse in the entire collection that is perhaps more attractive than Harb, son of Bint Helwa.

Another mare brought from Arabia by Lady Anne Blunt that should be mentioned was Basilisk, a grey Seglawieh Jedranieh of the strain of Ibn ed Derri. Basilisk was bought by the Duke of Westminster for breeding to thoroughbred horses, and produced for him some winners of races in the best of company.

Wild Thyme, a bay mare foaled 1876, which they bought of the Baggara tribe of the Euphrates, was the only animal secured by either the Blunts or Upton,

*The name given to Beteyen's mare by the Blunts.

ANTIKA, 4 YEARS

Dam—Asfura, daughter of Queen of Sheba (Betteyan's mare)
Sire—Mesaoud

of the coveted family of Ras el Fedawi, to
which belonged the famous Darley Arabian. It has often been stated that he
was a Manekhi Hedruj. Both Major
Upton and Lady Anne Blunt say he was
Ras el Fedawi. This is one of the sub-
families of Keheilet Ajuz, and the nearest
Major Upton was able to secure was the
bay mare Kesia, a Keheilet of Nowak,
closely akin to the Ras el Fedawi. Upton
says (Gleanings page 324): "Of the
strain called Ras el Fedawi, of which
family I understand was the Darley
Arabian, we saw some mares in another
tribe and in the hands of single Arabs,
but I do not remember to have seen any
in the Sabäah." The only one he could
buy was so badly broken down that he
would not take her.

Wild Thyme was bred to Kars, a bay
Seglawi Jedran horse of the Ibn Sbeni
strain, purchased at Aleppo by Mr. Blunt,
and considered of very choice blood.
Lady Anne Blunt ranks him as one of the
most valuable horses they secured. The

offspring was Raschida, a very remarkable mare, still owned (1906) by Hon. Miss Dillon, who bought her, with Hagar, and Jedrania, besides other choice animals, from the Blunts.

Raschida is a bay mare, foaled 1883, a Ras el Fedawi, 15 hands high. She has won nineteen jumping prizes, besides one second prize in the hunter class at Blanford. She carried 13 stone (182 ℔s) in the hunting field ten weeks before foaling, and is the only pure Arab mare in the Hunters' Improvement Stud Book, besides being registered in Weatherby's "General Stud Book," Vol. XV.

*Offspring of Raschida.*

1. 1887, b. m. Rommia, by El Emir.
2. 1889, b. m. Rakusheh, El Emir.
3. 1890, b. m. Rahatlakoum, by Gomussa.
4. 1891, b. m. Aziza, by El Emir.
5. 1893, b. h. Rasoul, by Imam.
6. 1894, b. m. Laili, by Jamrood.
7. 1895, b. h. Ras el Fedawi, by Havilah.
8. 1896, ch. f. (dead), by Volomel.
9. 1897, b. m. Riad, by Hail.
10. 1898, b. m. Raz-za-za, by Imamzada.
11. 1904, b. m. Mahal, by Imamzada.
12. 1905, b. m. Nessa, by Hauran.

RASCHIDA

Jedrania also proved one of the very valuable producers among the Arab mares of England. She was foaled in 1875, a Seglawi Jedranieh, bred by Ali Aga of Milich, at Deyr Hafa, on the Euphrates. Her dam was captured in war and given as a bribe to Ali Aga the Turkish-Pasha of Deyr, in whose possession she foaled Jedrania. From him the mare was purchased by Mr. Blunt.

*Offspring of Jedrania.*

1. 1881, ch, h. Jamschyd, by Abeyan el Khush.
2. 1882, ch. h. (dead) by Pharaoh.
3. 1884, b. m. Jebel Druz, by Kars.
4. 1885, b. m. Juniper, by Kars.
5. 1886, b. m. (dead), by Abeyran.
6. 1887, b. m. (dead), by Nizam.
7. 1888, b. m. Jedran, by El Emir.
8. 1891, b. h. (dead), Jebel Shammar.
9. 1893, b. h. Jezail, by Imam.
10. 1894, b. h. Jadoo, by Jamrood.
11. 1896, br. m. Yasimeen, by Imamzada.
12. 1898, b. h. Jezza, by Rasoul.

These are some of the fine mares that have been owned in England through the efforts of a few enthusiastic and persistent breeders. It will be noted

that they have produced sufficiently to
account for King Edward's dominion
being the source whence many other
countries have been able to supply themselves with pure Arab blood.

A number of the choicest stallions also
were brought by the Blunts, some from
Arabia, others from the Abbas Pasha
Stud, still others from Bombay. Among
the best of the first was Kars, a very
beautiful and impressive animal. Weatherby thus records him in Vol XIV of the
General Stud Book:

"Kars, a bay horse (foaled 1874) a
Seglawi Jedran of the Ibn Sbeni, pur-
chased at Aleppo by W. S. Blunt, from
Mahmoud Aga, chief of the irregulars.
This blood is considered the best in the
Syrian Desert."

Mesaoud is also a very choice Seglawi
Jedran horse of Ibn Sudan's strain of the
Roala Anazah, bred by Ali Pasha Sherif
from a mare bought in the desert by
Abbas Pasha. He won many prizes in
England and on the continent, his blood

MESAOUD

saturates the animals now at Crabbet Park, and he was purchased in 1903 by the Russian Government for use in the Imperial Stud.

Rataplan was bought by Mr. Blunt in Bombay. Visiting India in 1882 to see the great races for Arab horses which had become established events in that country, he recognised in Rataplan a horse he had seen ridden in Arabia by Jedäan ibu Mahaid of whom mention has been made. Inquiry proved his identification accurate, the horse had been brought to Bombay by Abdur Rhaman after Jedäan's death, and was raced successfully, winning the following events:

*Wellington,* May 15, 1882, Arab Handicap, 1½ miles, 500 Rs., beating Snowdrop, Ruby, and Copenhagen.

*Bangalore,* July 18, 1882, Arabian Purse, 1½ miles, 500 Rs., beating Dictator, Copenhagen and Khusroo.

*Bangalore,* July 22, 1882, Winner's Handicap, 1¾ miles, 500 Rs., beating Dictator, Grey Warrior, Euphrates, and Copenhagen.

*Baroda,* Dec. 28, 1882, Gaekwar's Purse, 1½ miles, 800 Rs., beating Blotting Paper, Robin Grey, Duchess, Slug, Morar, Redoubt, and Reserved.

Mr. Blunt then bought Rataplan and shipped him to England for use in the Crabbet Stud.

Many other Arab horses greatly distinguished themselves in racing in India; but as they never came to England or the Continent of Europe have left no influence upon modern occidental horse breeding. A rapid enumeration is all the attention that can be given them in the present writing.

Greyleg won 51 races at Bombay, Mysore, and Bangalore between 1861 and 1868. Hermit won 34 races during the same period. Rex, Euclid, and Lanercost were also great winners. The demand for anything that could win races from the rich Rajahs who made racing their pastime, caused standing offers of fabulous prices at all times by British officers, and the demand brought a partial supply. In 1893 not less than 16,000 rupees were added to the stakes at the Calcutta meeting alone. To win such prizes the Maharajah of Cooch Behar paid R5,000 ($2,500)

GREYLEG

EUCLID

LANERCOST

BLITZ

for Dominant, and R11,000 for Good
Hope, while R30,000 were offered and
refused for either Rex or Blitz. This
last-named horse was certainly one of the
greatest stake winners for his inches that
the world has ever seen. Bought originally by Lieut. O'Farrell of the 6th Dra-
goons for R400 ($200) he *never was
beaten*. After winning the Civil Service
Cup for the second time, his owner and
partners bought him in no less than fourteen pools, whose actual aggregate value
was $60,000. Later, he was bought by
Lord William Beresford, and used in the
stud in England, to a limited degree.
Afterward he passed into the possession
of the Maharajah of Patiala, who took
him back to India and used him for breeding. He is described by one who knew
him well, in these words:

"He is for his size, the most remarkable animal ever foaled. He is milk white
with black muzzle, which can be put in
a pint pot. Weight makes no difference
to him."

Another remarkable horse, who must be rated in the same class with Blitz, was Kismet. He was foaled in the desert in 1877, a Manakhi Hedruj, and taken to India by Abdur Rhaman, in 1882. In 1883–'84 he swept everything before him on the race track, never losing a race or heat, his total winnings for those seasons in India amounting to £30,000 ($150,000).

*Kismet's Races in India*

*Bangalore,* July 12, 1883, the Mysore Cup, 1¼ miles, carrying 139 lbs.

*Bangalore,* July 14, 1883, the Mysore Purse, 1½ miles, carrying 134 lbs.

*Bangalore,* July 19, 1883, Aga Khan's Purse, 1½ miles, carrying 134 lbs.

*Poonah,* Sept. 8, 1883, Aga Khan's Plate, 1¼ miles, carrying 126 lbs.

*Poonah,* Sept. 11, 1883, Aga Khan's Purse, 1¾ miles, carrying 131 lbs.

*Hyderabad,* Nov. 22, 1883 Deccan Handicap, 1½ miles, carrying 119 lbs.

*Bombay,* Feb. 12, 1884, The Derby, 1½ miles carrying 136 lbs.

*Bombay,* Feb. 14, 1884, Aga Khan's Purse, 1½ miles, carrying 133 lbs

Immediately after this race Lieut. Broadwood brought Kismet to England,

KISMET

A TYPICAL POLO PONY.   SIRE, KISMET

where he was owned by Col. R. D. Coyn-
ingham V. C. He landed after a tem-
pestuous voyage in the latter part of
April, and so confident was his owner
of his prowess, that he matched him to
run against Asil, without training, at
Newmarket. Asil beat him in this race
for the only time in Kismet's entire career.
Twice afterward Kismet turned the
tables on Asil, showing that it was lack of
condition that lost him his first race with
that horse. In 1885 Kismet was ridden
at Newmarket by Fred Archer, who rode
the Derby winner five different times,
and he pronounced Kismet the gamest
horse he ever rode. Such, also, was the
opinion of Wood, who rode him in his
races against Asil at Newmarket and
Sandown Park. Both these races were
for two miles, and Kismet won "hands
down," carrying 126 pounds. After that he
was bought by Hon. John Corbett, M. P.,
as a saddle horse, and he sold him to Rev.
F. F. Vidal, who kept him in the stud until
1891, when he leased him to Mr. Ran-

dolph Huntington, of Oyster Bay, Long Island. After a long and stormy passage Kismet reached New York by Str. *Canada*, Nov, 11, 1891, only to die two hours after landing, of pleuro-pneumonia contracted on the voyage. This rather extended history of Kismet has been given because, though his untimely death was so serious a loss, he has had, and will continue to have, an important influence on horse breeding in America, two of his pure bred sons having come to this country in 1893, as will be noted later.

Maidan is the last of the great horses that came to England from Arabia through India, whose name can have our especial attention. Many who knew him, including Lady Anne Blunt and the Hon. Miss Dillon, place him even above Kismet, and the opinion is concurred in by others who knew him only by his offspring. Maidan was foaled in 1869 in Nejd, a chestnut (as was Kismet), said by some to have been a Manakhi Hedruj, though

MAIDAN AT 23

this was doubted by others because of his great beauty, the Manakhi being a family of rather plain appearance, though great race horses. He was brought to Bombay by Abdur Rhaman in 1871, and sold to Captain Johnstone, who immediately commenced racing him, though the colt was but two years old. Captain Fisher and Major Brough were also interested in Maidan; and as these English officers had tested him they were free in taking the long odds which were laid against him by the Australian sports who came to the races and were ready to lay against an untried colt. It is said that after Maidan won the Punjab Cup, the Australians had hardly money enough left to pay their passage home. For three years, from 1871 to 1874, Maidan continued his winning career, until no further matches could be made for him. Then, at 5 years of age, he was sold to Lieut. Col. Brownlow of the 72d Highlanders, as a charger. Brownlow was a heavyweight of nineteen stone (266 lbs.)

with his equipment, yet Maidan carried
him for twelve years in campaigns
through the mountainous regions of India
and Afghanistan, until the soldier was
killed in the fight at Kandahar, at the
end of the famous forced march of Lord
Roberts's Army from Cabul, three hundred miles distant. After carrying
Brownlow for ten years Maidan won the
Ganges Hog Hunt Cup, and also a four
mile steeplechase across difficult country.
At seventeen years of age, on the death of
Brownlow, Maidan was bought by Lord
Airlie who again put him to racing where
he won a number of races both on the
flat and steeplechases. He was then sold
to Captain the Hon. Eustace Vesey, who
bought him to take to England. Leaving
India on the troopship *Jumna* Maidan
got as far as Suez, where the ship met
the expedition going to the relief of
Suakim, where Osman Digna was har-
rassing the garrison, and was pressed into
service as a transport for troops to Mas-
sowah, near the lower end of the Red Sea.

MAIDAN AT 23 YEARS OF AGE POSING FOR HIS PORTRAIT

So it happened that the old race horse and charger had his journey lengthened, to the degree that *he stood on his feet one hundred days* without once lying down, before he reached Marseilles. Yet Capt. Vesey raced him successfully at Pau, and afterward in England. He won a steeple-chase when twenty-two years of age. When he had to be destroyed, because of a broken leg, at twenty-three, he was absolutely sound. In 1890 he was de-scribed in the London *Live Stock Journal*, as "fresh and well, with immense bone below the knee (he measured eight inches) and as clean in the legs as a four year old, notwithstanding the fact that he was hunted in Suffolk last year."

He was a very beautiful horse, the finest type of a high caste Arab, fifteen hands high. Maidan's blood is also to be found in the United States, though the U. S. Department of Agriculture decided that his daughter, from a pure-bred Ras al Fedawi Arab mare, and registered as thoroughbred in Weather-

bey's "General Stud Book," also, present-
ing the certificate of Weatherbey & Sons,
must pay duty, *because the sire and dam
of Maidan were not so registered*, though
Maidan himself had been accepted and
registered.   The reason his sire and dam
were not registered was that they lived
and died in Nejd, and there was no
occasion for them to be registered at the
English Jockey Club.

HEIRESS AND HALF-BRED DAUGHTER, 4 MONTHS OLD

# CHAPTER V

## ARAB HORSES IN AMERICA

CONTRARY to generally accepted opinion, many good Arabs have come to America, even from the early days. It cannot be doubted that they have imparted their good qualities to some of our most useful horses, the influence of Arab blood being especially noticeable in the old Morgans, that of the Barb in the descendants of Henry Clay.

General Washington's famous grey charger was an entire son of the desert-born horse Ranger, imported to New London, Connecticut, about 1765. He was a dapple grey, fifteen hands high, of the finest form, symmetry, and finish. As Washington was six feet, three inches tall, and weighed more than two hundred pounds, it is evident that the little son of Ranger must have been a weight carrier.

It is related that Washington had his
attention attracted to the superiority of
the horses ridden by the Connecticut
cavalry when he took command of the
Continental army at Boston. Calling
"Light Horse Harry Lee" into his coun-
sels, they found that these were sons and
daughters of Ranger. Captain Lindsay
was thereupon sent to the Connecticut
valley to purchase the horse, and he was
taken to Virginia where he was afterward known as the Lindsay Arabian.
The horse that General Israel Putnam
rode when he galloped down the steep
declivity of a hundred steps at Green-
wich, Connecticut, later in the war, so
escaping the British, was own brother to
Washington's charger.

The four famous grey stallions that drew
Lady Washington's coach to Philadelphia
when Congress convened, were bred on
the Washington plantation at Mount
Vernon, and were half-bred Arabians.

In the first volume of "Bruce's American Stud Book" we find a list of no less

than forty-two Arab horses imported
into the United States during the century
between 1760 and 1860, besides twelve
Arab mares, four Barb horses, and two
Barb mares. Since that time the number
has been increased greatly.

Mention has already been made of the
Keene Richards importations. It was
in 1854–'55 that he was induced to go
to Arabia for horses, backed by the New
Orleans Jockey Club, accompanied by
Troyon, the animal painter, who was to
assist him in making his selections. He
went among the Anazah tribes and
brought back with him some very valuable animals of the choicest families. In
this country they failed of the recognition they deserved for many reasons,
one being the unfortunate time of their
arrival. The great Civil War was brewing,
and people had their attention drawn to
more serious questions than horse breeding in 1857, when the Keene Richards
Arabs reached Kentucky. The best of
his horses was bred to but five mares, yet

one of them produced the great race horse
Limestone, and another the dam of Dor-
sey's Golddust.    General W. T. Withers,
one of the most successful breeders of
trotters in Kentucky, had two or three
mares in his stud sired by one of the Keene
Richards Arabs, that he considered the
choicest of any he had.    In 1861 the Civil
War burst upon the land, and the Keene
Richards's Arabs were scattered and lost,
as were other valuable animals of other
breeds.

It is told that after the battle of Pitts-
burgh Landing (Shiloh) the Confederate
General Breckenridge went to George-
town, Kentucky, to Mr. Richards, begging
conveyance to Virginia as quickly as
possible, as the Federal troops were pur-
suing him.    Richards had nothing to offer
but a pair of three year old half-bred
Arab fillies.    These he hitched to a buck-
board and started.    The Federals pur-
sued on thoroughbred horses, but though
they gained for a while, their bolt was
soon shot, and they had to draw rein.

The Arab fillies never stopped until they had Breckenridge safely within the Confederate lines. It is doubtful if he would have proved a good witness for the case of those who prate about the failure of the Keene Richards's Arabs.

Other notable Arabian horses that came to America were the two, Mäaneke Hedragi and Siklany Gidran (note these names), sent as a present to Hon. Wm. H. Seward when Lincoln's Secretary of State, Umbark, sent to President Van Buren, Linden Tree and Leopard, presented by the Sultan of Turkey Abdul Hamid II., to General U. S. Grant. The so-called Arabs or Barbs brought to New York in 1905, said to be intended as a present for President Roosevelt, need no attention. They were a fraud. Mr. Roosevelt would have none of them, and when sold by auction to pay their feed bills at Hoboken, they did not bring the value of the oats they had eaten. It is such beasts as they, when called Arabs, that

discredit the entire race with the un-
informed.

Mention has not been made of a con-
siderable consignment of Arabians, both
mares and stallions, brought over by
Commodore Jesse D. Elliott, U. S. N.,
in 1838. They were procured by him
during a cruise to the coast of Syria in
1837, on the frigate *Constitution*. They
are registered in Bruce's American Stud
Book, but the disposition made of them
is not noted.

Since 1885 quite a number of really
high - caste Arabs have come to the
United States. Naomi, foaled in Upton's
stable in England, her dam brought
from Arabia on his first visit, was imported in 1888. She was a very valuable
mare, well known and esteemed in England. The list of Naomi's offspring has
already been given. She greatly en-
riched the horse breeding of America by
her blood, and died full of years and
honours.

In 1893 Mr. Huntington bought Nazli,

GARAVEEN

daughter of Naomi and Maidan. She
is still owned by the Huntington Stud
at Oyster Bay, and has produced some
most valuable animals. Two of these, a
son and a daughter, both by her half-
brother Anazah (son of Naomi and Gen.
Grant's Leopard) are owned by Mr.
Herman Hoopes, of Philadelphia. Mr.
Huntington also imported on same ship
with Nazli, two pure bred sons of Kismet,
Nimr, son of Nazli, and Garaveen, whose
dam was Kushdil, another daughter
of Naomi, Kushdil's sire having been
Kars.

Garaveen was bought by Mr. J. A P.
Ramsdell of Newburgh, who also bought
Ras Aloula and Rakusheh from Miss
Dillon, and Shahwan from Mr. W. S.
Blunt. He also secured a white mare
from an Arab Sheik who brought her
to the Columbian Exposition at Chicago
in 1893. Her breeding is not known, and
she lacks registration; yet Nejme bears
every indication of being a high caste
Arab mare.

This, however, is by no means a safe
way to judge of a horse's breeding. A
chestnut mare by Maidan, imported from
England by the writer in 1898, has the
most perfect conformation and courage,
such as would cause her to be judged a
pure-bred Arab in the choicest company.
No other son or daughter of Maidan can
surpass her in beauty of head, loftily
carried tail, perfect form and symmetry.
Yet she is only a half-bred Arab; her dam
was a thoroughbred English racing mare.
She has distinguished herself in the hunting fields of England, France, Algeria,
America, won first prize in jumping at
the Crystal Palace, London, in 1896, and
has bred eight beautiful foals. If appearance and performance were all that
need be sought for as credentials, Heiress
would pass for a pure-bred Arab of the
very highest type. If further evidence
were needed that appearance is not always a safe ground for judging a horse to
be pure-bred, a son of Garaveen owned
by Mr. Ramsdell, whose dam was a polo

HEIRESS

Daughter of Maidan ; her dam a thoroughbred mare by Herbertstown
Seventeen years old, has hunted in England, France, Algeria, America.  First
prize in jumping class at Crystal Palace, London, 1896.  Dam of 8 foals

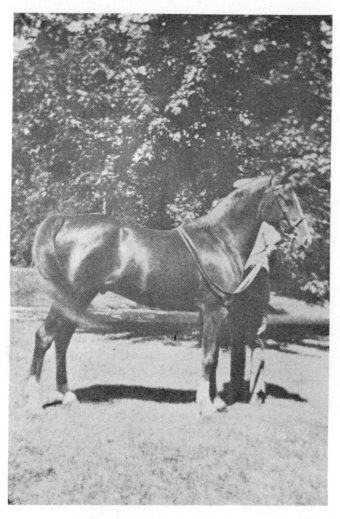

HALF-BRED GELDING BY GARAVEEN

pony mare, and in the same stable with Nejme, may also be cited. Nothing could be more beautiful than this chestnut gelding, yet we know that he is but a half-bred.

Speaking of the necessity for care in making certain of the origin of horses claiming to be pure bred Arabians, Lady Anne Blunt writes:

"As it is a fundamental principle at the Crabbet Arabian Stud that no stallion, however individually excellent, is eligible for service if there is any doubt *or lack of information* as to a true Arabian descent, it follows that at this stud any 'not proven' element must remain an insuperable objection. I have heard of disastrous results from the neglect of this rule, for example from Prince Sangusco, who told me of the immense trouble he had to eliminate the blood of horses he had accepted on insufficient testimony.

"On the other hand there are cases where, the risk having been run, results have justified the experiment, as any flaw in blood is sure to come out in descendants sooner or later, and if results are persistently good they may practically be treated as proof.   But that takes years."

Mr. W. S. Forbes, of Boston, about the same time, brought two Arabs, the chestnut mare Jamilla and the bay stallion Bedr, from the Crabbet Arabian Stud, with the great race horse Meddler, to this country. Hon. W. C. Whitney also imported a bay horse from Bombay somewhat later, and Mr. Eustis got the bay mares Bushra and Backaret from Mr. Blunt in 1900.

In 1898 there came from Miss Dillon's Pudlicote Stud the two mares Raksh and Shabaka.   The former was a most beautiful animal, a daughter of Maidan, her dam by El Emir from Rachida, and so of the much prized Ras al Fedawi strain.   Her death, leaving no progeny, was a serious loss.   Shabaka was bred by Lord Arthur Cecil, her sire the Duke of Bedford's Mameluke, her dam Mr. Chaplin's Kesia II, already mentioned in

RAKSH

SEGARIO, 4 YEARS

Bred, owned and ridden by the author

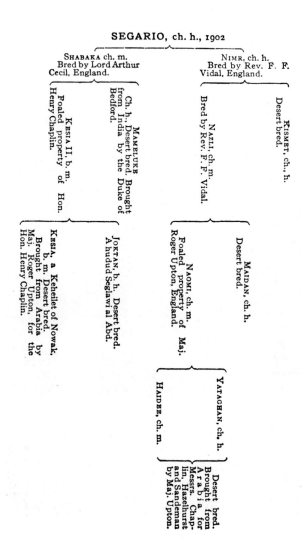

SEGARIO, ch. h., 1902

SHABAKA ch. m.
Bred by Lord Arthur
Cecil, England.

NIMR, ch. h.
Bred by Rev. F. F.
Vidal, England.

KISMET, ch. h.
Desert bred.

MAMELUKE
Ch. h., Desert bred. Brought
from India by the Duke of
Bedford.

KESIA II, b. m.
Foaled property of Hon.
Henry Chaplin.

NAZLI, ch. m.
Bred by Rev. F. F. Vidal.

JOKTAN, b. h. Desert bred.
A hudud Seglawi al Abd.

KESIA, a Keheilet of Nowak,
b. m. Desert bred.
Brought from Arabia by
Maj. Roger Upton, for the
Hon. Henry Chaplin.

MAIDAN, ch. h.
Desert bred.

NAOMI, ch. m.
Foaled property of Maj.
Roger Upton, England.

YATAGHAN, ch. h.
Desert bred.
Brought from
Arabia, for
Messrs. Chap-
lin, Hazelhurst
and Sandeman
by Maj. Upton.

HAIDEE, ch. m.

connection with Major Upton's importations.

She is dam of the very beautiful
horse Segario, whose sire was Nimr. In
1905 Shabaka was sold to the proprietors
of the Huntington Stud, together with the
grand Russian Arab Gouniead, bred at
the Imperial Stud at Streletsky, and
sent to America by the Russian Government in 1893. Shabaka foaled a very
promising filly by Gouniead in February
1906.

In 1905 Miss Dillon sent the bay horse
Häil, a son of the famous mare Hagar.
Häil is 15.3. His sire was Jamrood,
son of Maidan and Jerud.

Two months after Häil, came the bay
stallion Imamzada, son of Imam and
Kesia II. Imam was a bay son of
El Emir, that Miss Dillon bought at
Damascus, a Manakhi ibu Sbeyli, and
Ishtar, a white mare, one of the first
bought in the desert by the Blunts. For
ten years Imamzada has been distinguished in the Midland Counties of

England, as a hunter and a sire of hunters.
He is about 15.2 and of immense bone,
measuring more than eight inches below
the knee. Imam also greatly distin-
quished himself in the hunting field with
the Heythorpe Hounds, calling forth
most laudatory notice in the London
sporting papers for his jumping, manners,
and endurance. At the Oxfordshire Show
he won a prize of £40 in a jumping con-
test, where he cleared six feet. He was
also a fine horse in harness. In the
autumn of 1894 Miss Dillon drove him
to Cirencestor Fair, twenty-eight miles,
in two hours and thirty-five minutes,
hitched to a heavy cart, in which were
Miss Dillon, and a groom, besides saddles
and rugs. Imam returned by another
route to Charlbury, the same day, thirty-
three miles, in three hours and five
minutes.

A notion of the service a good Arab
can perform may be gathered from the
record of Imam's doings in the eight days
beginning November 11, 1894:

IMAMZADA

### Imamzada, b. h., 1891

Bred by the Hon. Miss E. Dillon, England

KESIA II, b. m.
Foaled property of
Hon. Henry Chaplin.

IMAM, b. h.
Bred by Miss Dillon,
England.

*KESIA, a Keheilet of Nowak. Desert bred. Brought from Arabia by Maj. R. D. Upton for Hon. Henry Chaplin. England.

Hudud, SEGLAWI EL ABD. Desert bred.

ISHTAR, wh. m. Desert bred. Brought from Arabia by W. S. Blunt.

ELEMIR, b. h. Desert bred. Brought from Arabia by Hon. Miss Dillon.

\* Pedigree of Kesia as given by R. D. Upton's "Gleanings from the Desert of Arabia," p. 387.

4. Breed—a Keheilet of Nowak.
Her color, bay (red).
Breed of her sire—Dabeh Nowak.
In foal by the hudud Seglawi al Abd.
His tribe, *i. e.* the tribe of the horse, Ruallah Anazah.
17th Jammaz, (July) of the Christian year 1875.
The testifier of this writing is the Shaykh.
SULEYMAN IBN MIRSHED.

Seal of
Ibn [    ] Suleyman
Mirshed

ROSE OF SHARON
21 years old; dam of 13 foals

Saturday—Carried Edwards (Miss Dillon's Stud Groom) hunting, rider thirteen stone (182 lbs.)

Monday—Ridden to hounds to pilot Miss Roberts (daughter of Gen. Lord Roberts); out seven hours, with plenty of galloping and jumping.

Tuesday—Fourteen miles in harness at a fast pace.

Thursday—Thirty miles in harness.

Friday—harness again.

Saturday—Sixteen miles in harness.

At the outbreak of war in South Africa, Imam went as a charger. He was the only horse on the ship that stood the 6,000 mile voyage without apparent injury, and he served with distinction throughout the whole war.

In October 1905 there came also the famous old mare Rose of Sharon, a chestnut, foaled in 1885, her sire Hadban, dam Rodania, a Keheilet Ajuz of Ibn Rodan's strain, whose romantic history is mentioned in connection with the mares at Crabbet Park.

*Offspring of Rose of Sharon.*

1890, ch. h. Rafyk, by Azrak.

1891, ch. h. Rasham, by Azrak.

1892, ch. h. Ridaa by Merzuk.

1894, ch. m. Rishmeh, by Shahwan.

1894, ch. m Rotuba, by Ahmar.

1898, ch. m. Rayyana, by Ahmar.
1899, ch. m. Rebekdar, by Mesaoud.
1900, ch. h. Ras el Jeyr, by Mesaoud.
1901, ch. h. Rijin, by Mahruss.
1902, ch. m. Rumeliya, by Rejeb.
1906, ch. h. Rodam, by Harb, son of the "broken-legged mare."

The death of Raksh left no animal in America of the Ras el Fedawi family, and the only place where it was known to exist was in Miss Dillon's two old mares Raschida (24 yrs. old) and Rommia (19 yrs.). Rommia had failed to produce a foal for ten years. Raschida had by her side a beautiful bay filly by Hauran, and Miss Dillon also had a yearling daughter of Raschida (foal of 1904) by Imamzada. After much persuasion these were both secured, and safely reached America in October 1905. Raschina's breeding has been mentioned, also that of Imamzada. Hauran is a son of Hagar, his sire Jezail a son of Jedrania. The combination of blood in the younger filly, therefore, is not less choice than that of the older. They

RUMELIYA

Dam—Rose of Sharon, daughter of Rodania
Sire—Rejeb, son of Rosemary (also a daughter of Rodania) and Mesaoud

both unite the choicest strains of Major
Upton's importations, with the earlier
of the Blunts, and are believed to be the
only animals in America of the Ras al
Fedawi family.

In 1906 three more mares came from
Crabbett Park, (1) Rumeliya, 4 years, a
daughter of Rose of Sharon, her sire Rejeb,
son of Rosemary and Mesaoud—in foal by
Astraled, son of Queen of Sheba (Beteyan's mare); (2) Rosetta, 4 years—a daughter of Rosemary and Mesaoud—also in
foal by Astraled; and (3) Antika, 4 years
—daughter of Asfura, and grand-daugh-
ter of Queen of Sheba—in foal by Harb,
son of Bint Helwa (the broken-legged
mare) and Mesaoud. These three, combining the choicest strains of blood that
ever left Arabia, and joining the same
stud where are owned the Rose of Sharon
and two of Raschida's daughters, must
prove a valuable addition to the Arabs
in America.

# CHAPTER VI

## SOME LAST WORDS

NO PERSON who reads the books from which much of the information conveyed in these pages has been obtained can fail to be impressed with the idea that the blood of Keheilet Ajuz is a preponderating influence in the best Arab horses. The animals possessed of this blood are not a separate breed among Arabs—all pure Arabs are of one breed. But, as we know of the old Morgans in America, there were separate families, for example, Woodburys, Giffords, Bulrushes, and all were Morgans, so in Arab horses there is a choice; and of them all the descendants of Keheilet Ajuz are the first. Upton says in "Gleanings From the Desert" (p. 320):

"It appears to me that although there are numerous offshoots from the Keheilet

Ajuz, each with a specific name, there is still a main line or strain of descent carried on of Keheilet Ajuz without any distinguishing name, and that the name Keheilet Ajuz is sufficient to mark any such horse or mare."

He also explodes the tradition that mares are not to be had of the Arabs, and makes evident the fact that if a man knows what he wants, and has the money to pay the price; he can get it, or could at the time of his visits (p. p. 365-6).

"Before leaving this portion of the subject, it is convenient to allude to an assertion which has been made, and so oft repeated that it has been accepted as an established fact—that it is impossible to obtain an Arabian mare; that the Arabs will not part with a mare; that they will sell horses, but nothing will tempt them to part with a mare. The least informed on the subject of Arabians will tell you this as glibly and with as much assurance as if he had been brought up in the desert. One certainly announced that there was a law forbidding the export of an Arabian mare: Now, I

ROSETTA, 4 YEARS

Dam—Rosemary, daughter of Rodania
Sire—Mesaoud

can assure my readers that it is not by any means impossible to obtain a genuine Arab mare. We visited the most exclusive of all Badaween tribes and never heard of such a law. If any law did exist, it would be against selling, not exporting; but we never heard of such a thing in the desert. I can assure my readers that among the genuine Badaween of the Arabian desert we found no prejudice against parting with or selling a mare. Difficulty there certainly is to induce such people as the Anazah to sell either horses or mares, for they do not traffic in horses; but if there be any difference, you might get a good mare with less trouble than a good horse.

" I have the best of possible authority for refuting the statement that mares are not to be got, for mares were not infrequently offered to us, and among the Anazah (not the wandering people of Erack) we obtained both mares and horses, and the former without more difficulty than the latter."

The idea has also been given currency that Manakhi Hedruj was a strain so rare as to be seldom seen in these days, was no longer to be had even for large sums of money, and that they are always chestnuts, of a size so much above the other Arab families that these others are merely "pony Arabs."

Upton says of them (Gleanings p. 321):

"The Manakhi appeared to us a favourite strain, for both horses and mares of this family are to be found in most tribes of the Badaween; and we thought, with the exception of Keheilet Ajuz, there were more horses and mares among the Anazah, certainly among the Sabäah, of the Manakhi family than any other."

The Blunts, four years after Upton, had no difficulty in securing several animals of the Manakhi family, which they brought with them to the Crabbet Arabian Stud. Of their colour and size Upton remarks (Gleanings p. 321):

"There was a nice clean-made, lengthy, useful, and racing-like *dark grey* three year old filly of the Manakhi Hedruj family which belonged to Shaykh Jedäan ibn Mahaid. There were four mares of Suleiman ibn Mirshid picketed in front of his tent, the best of which he considered to be the *bluish-grey* (Azzrak) mare, four or five years old. She was also of the Manakhi Hedruj family, and stood *fourteen hands, three inches high.*"

Speaking of colour of Arab horses he says (p. 341):

"As to colour, I do not pretend to restrict it; but among the Anazah bay appeared to us the most general, and, I think is the favourite colour among the Arabs; chestnuts and greys are less numerous, and together would not equal the number of those of a bay colour."

Finally, the question seems pertinent— Why, if Arab horses are so valuable, their value so well known, and they can be procured, have they not become more widely distributed?

Various answers, all good, may be given to this question. In the first place the average horseman has come to believe their qualities and reputation to be figments of the imagination, like the Arabian Nights tales, and having similar origin. He has never seen one of these wonderful horses, and none of his friends have seen one. Therefore, the horse as he is represented does not exist. Again, even if he becomes convinced there is such a horse he does not know where to look for him, does not feel certain he can secure the genuine article if he parts with his good money to obtain one, and if he does find what he becomes convinced is what he wants the price is sure to be a stiff one. The fact is the whole business involves the question of supply and demand, which is the key to all economic calculations.

From this time forward it will pay less and less to breed anything but the best horses, and those which will yield the safest return will be such as will be best adapted for use under the saddle, either for pleasure or as cavalry mounts. In either of those forms of utility no horse that ever lived can compare with one of

Arab blood, and the supply of animals of that kind is extremely limited. The people possessing them, whether the Bedouins or those who have bought from them, have never had an over supply.

A reason for this is perhaps to be found in one statement of conditions for which Mr. Wilfrid Blunt is authority namely: that the pure Arab is not a prolific breeding animal. He thinks one cause for this may be his intense inbreeding. Inbreeding is the only way to secure fixity of type in any form of animal life; but the penalty carried with it is limitation of the reproductive tendency. Mr. Blunt informed one inquirer that if fifteen mares out of twenty-five produced offspring each year at Crabbett Park, he felt satisfied.

The tendency of this condition of affairs is to make the supply of pure Arabs always short, and the price high. A careful study of the lists presented to the readers of this book, however, will show that certain mares have been consistent and uniform producers of numerous and valuable offspring. By acquiring, therefore, from breeders of reputation, animals whose history has been so well defined as to admit them into authoritative records such as Weatherbey's General Stud Book, and the American Jockey Club Stud Book, selecting carefully among them such as are of the choicest strains and those coming from long lived and prolific families—for such are certainly to be had—it is possible to secure the means of breeding horses that shall be both a pleasure and a profit to the breeder.

# COMMENTS ON THE CRABBET STUD

Crabbet Park is located in Sussex, England, thirty-five miles from London. It was founded by Wilfred Scawen Blunt and Lady Anne Blunt, and sustained until 1957 by their daughter, Lady Wentworth.

In the early years of the stud a bi-annual sale was held which was always a much noted occasion throughout the horse world. On such an occasion in 1902 Mr. Blunt is quoted as saying, "It was the conviction that this wonderful breed of horses was threatened with extinction in the native home that led me, twenty-five years ago, to make the attempt you see carried out at Crabbet of rescuing at least a fraction of the race and preserving it in all its purity in England. This was my first and most important object-- not to improve the breed--for it really needs no improvement--but to keep it pure; pure not only in blood, but in type also, to preserve it carefully from deterioration in shape, in temper, in hardihood, and from departure from those special characteristics of beauty which are peculiar to the ancient race.

During the early years of the Crabbet Stud there were generally about one hundred and fifty Arabian horses kept on the premises, including the fillies and colts. The annual sales as well as sales by private treaty served for years as a fountainhead for the establishment of studs in many countries throughout the world. Following is a list of horses imported to the United States during the Crabbet Stud heydays.

| YEAR | SEX | NAME | IMPORTER |
|------|-----|------|----------|
| 1893 | S | Bedr 239 | William H. Forbes |
| 1893 | M | Jamila 240 | William H. Forbes |
| 1900 | S | Ibn Mahruss 22 | Mr. Eustis |
| 1900 | M | Bushra 23 | Mr. Eustis |
| 1905 | M | Shibine 160 | F. Lothrop Ames |
| 1905 | M | Rose of Sharon 246 | Spencer Borden |
| 1906 | M | Antika 162 | Spencer Borden |
| 1906 | S | Razzia 202 | Spencer Borden |
| 1906 | M | Rosetta 245 | Spencer Borden |
| 1906 | M | Rumeliya 247 | Spencer Borden |
| 1906 | S | Rodan 258 | Spencer Borden |

| YEAR | SEX | NAME | IMPORTER |
|------|-----|------|----------|
| 1907 | M | Markisa 24 | Homer Davenport |
| 1909 | S | Astraled 238 | F. Lothrop Ames |
| 1910 | M | Narda II 164 | F. Lothrop Ames |
| 1910 | S | Crabbet 309 | F. Lothrop Ames |
| 1910 | S | Berid 80 | Homer Davenport |
| 1910 | S | Jahil 81 | Homer Davenport |
| 1910 | S | Hauran 197 | Spencer Borden |
| 1911 | M | Risalda 165 | Spencer Borden |
| 1911 | M | Rosa Rugosa 166 | Spencer Borden |
| 1911 | M | Radha 284 | Spencer Borden |
| 1918 | S | Berk 343 | W.R. Brown |
| 1918 | M | Baraza 344 | W.R. Brown |
| 1918 | M | Battla 345 | W.R. Brown |
| 1918 | M | Rijma 346 | W.R. Brown |
| 1918 | M | Ramla 347 | W.R. Brown |
| 1918 | M | Romim 348 | W.R. Brown |
| 1918 | M | Rishrash 349 | W.R. Brown |
| 1918 | S | Rajafan 350 | W.R. Brown |
| 1918 | M | Rokhsa 351 | W.R. Brown |
| 1918 | M | Kasima 352 | W.R. Brown |
| 1918 | M | Kerbela 353 | W.R. Brown |
| 1918 | M | Nueyra 354 | W.R. Brown |
| 1918 | M | Numera 355 | W.R. Brown |
| 1918 | S | Nafia 356 | W.R. Brown |
| 1918 | M | Rasna 357 | W.R. Brown |
| 1918 | M | Simawa 358 | W.R. Brown |
| 1918 | M | Felestin 359 | W.R. Brown |
| 1919 | S | Rizvan 381 | W.R. Brown |
| 1924 | M | Ana 518 | Albert W. Harris |
| 1926 | M | Ferdisia 595 | W.K. Kellogg |
| 1926 | M | Ferda 596 | W.K. Kellogg |
| 1926 | S | Raseyn 597 | W.K. Kellogg |
| 1926 | M | Rossana 598 | W.K. Kellogg |
| 1926 | S | Rimal 599 | W.K. Kellogg |
| 1926 | M | Raida 600 | W.K. Kellogg |
| 1926 | M | Rifla 601 | W.K. Kellogg |
| 1926 | M | Rasafa 602 | W.K. Kellogg |
| 1926 | M | Bahreyn 603 | W.K. Kellogg |
| 1926 | S | Nasik 604 | W.K. Kellogg |
| 1926 | M | Rifda 605 | W.K. Kellogg |
| 1926 | M | Rasima 606 | W.K. Kellogg |
| 1926 | S | Raswan 607 | W.K. Kellogg |
| 1926 | M | Bint 608 | W.K. Kellogg |
| 1926 | S | Razam 612 | W.K. Kellogg |

| YEAR | SEX | NAME | IMPORTER |
|------|-----|------|----------|
| 1926 | S | Ferdin 613 | W.K. Kellogg |
| 1927 | M | Farasin 615 | W.K. Kellogg |
| 1928 | S | Mirzam 808 | Roger A. Selby |
| 1928 | M | Kareyma 811 | Roger A. Selby |
| 1928 | M | Indaia 813 | Roger A. Selby |
| 1928 | M | Rifala 815 | Roger A. Selby |
| 1930 | M | Kiyama 809 | Roger A. Selby |
| 1930 | M | Hilwe 810 | Roger A. Selby |
| 1930 | M | Selmnab 812 | Roger A. Selby |
| 1930 | M | Raselma 814 | Roger A. Selby |
| 1930 | M | Jerama 819 | Roger A. Selby |
| 1930 | M | Namilla 855 | Roger A. Selby |
| 1930 | M | Rasmina 856 | Roger A. Selby |
| 1930 | M | Rose of France 857 | Roger A. Selby |
| 1932 | S | Rahal 950 | Roger A. Selby |
| 1932 | S | Selmian 951 | Roger A. Selby |
| 1932 | S | Raffles 952 | Roger A. Selby |
| 1932 | S | Menzil 953 | Roger A. Selby |
| 1932 | M | Rishafieh 954 | Roger A. Selby |
| 1933 | M | Rimini 973 | Roger A. Selby |
| 1933 | S | Nureddin 974 | Roger A. Selby |
| 1940 | M | Indian Dawn 1875 | Frederick L. Wehr |
| 1940 | M | Crown of India 1876 | Frederick L. Wehr |
| 1940 | S | Rosanthus 1877 | Fredereck L Wehr |

It has been an excellent group of horses imported over the years to the United States from the Crabbet Stud. Lady Wentworth was painfully aware of this as she wrote in **Horses in the Making** (1951), "Even Arabia can produce no finer Arabians now than those bred here. We have just reason to be proud of all this. We must, however, beware lest we lose our hard-won supremacy and allow the war and the freehanded and clever American breeders and other buyers to skim the cream from our stock."

William E. Jones
Fort Collins, Colorado
1973

# CRABBET ARABIAN STUD, 1924

*(Founded in the last Century).*

## The Purest and most Authentic Blood of Arabia.

**No Connection with any Arab Society.**

*Press Photo Agency.*

CHAMPION SKOWRONEK

Address THE MANAGER,
Care of THE RT. HON. LADY WENTWORTH,
CRABBET PARK, POUNDHILL, WORTH, SUSSEX

Telegrams
WENTWORTH, POUNDHILL, SUSSEX

Telephone :
22 POUNDHILL

Station :
THREE BRIDGES (1½ miles)

CRABBET PARK

CHAMPION MESAOUD—Type in 1885.                 *Photo: Rouch.*

CHAMPION RASIM—Present Day.              *Press Photo Agency*

THE GRAND CHAMPION OF AUSTRALIA.    (Sire, Rafyk: Dam, Rose of Jericho.)

# Crabbet Arabian Stud.

RUSTEM.

THE high caste Arab is exceedingly rare, and his wonderful beauty of form and carriage puts him in a class apart from everything but the highest type of English Thoroughbred, of which he is an ancestor, and which owes its quality and beauty to him, Cicero, Bend Or, and Cyllene being almost pure Arabian in type. Mr. Prior has shown that the best Thoroughbred foundation stock in the female line was of almost entirely pure Eastern blood, and that all the T.B.'s in the world are descended from three pure Eastern sires in the male line. The terms "Turk" and "Barb," were often used for horses whose pictures show them to have been high caste Arabians, and we have Mr. Blunt's authority for stating that seventy years ago the Arab was scheduled to give the Barb 12 lbs. to 14 lbs. in racing. In France, America, Austria, Italy, and India, the Arab and Anglo-Arab cross is thoroughly established for producing the best hunters and cavalry horses, and most foreign governments fully recognise the value of Arab blood. Our own hunter, polo, and harness horse breeders should take every chance of introducing Arab blood, but Arab must not include Syrian or Barb, which are both inferior races. The Arab is a natural.bold and fearless jumper, and the brilliance of his trotting action is one of the best tests of his caste, but it must be insisted on that the high caste Arabian is the only eastern horse of real value, and few people have ever seen him at all outside Nejd. The ordinary second rate animal so common in the East will often have an excellent individual record for work, due to his admixture of real Arab blood, but he will never be a successful sire, and in England we are chiefly familiar with this class of eastern horse, for whom the vague words "imported" or

SEYAL. From Picture by Lady Anne Blunt.

# THE CRABBET STUD  145

"desert bred" or "from the tribes" cover a multitude of unknown and undesirable ancestors; yet these are accepted wholesale as "pure Arabs," and the confusion of Syrians, Egyptians and Barbs grows daily worse and worse.

The Crabbet Arabian Stud was founded towards the middle of the last century from the purest authenticated strains in Arabia, imported by Mr. and Lady Anne Blunt. It has been carried on with the strictest attention to purity and excellence of blood, and can be relied on as the best and most specialised pedigree stock in existence. Great confusion has been created by legendary myths, and the hasty conclusions of pseudo scientific and other writers with no practical knowledge of horses or of Arabia, combined by the constant importation to England of low caste and mongrel types entirely despised in the East as common drudges, but actually used in England as stallions, to the great astonishment of oriental visitors. Breeders are warned not to accept as Arabian anything which is of unknown pedigree and origin. The extreme antiquity of the breed makes it essential that it should be in no way contaminated.

Crabbet has always been unique in its attention to pure blood, and the history of every horse was verified over a course of years by Lady Anne Blunt with her Beduin friends from the tribes of origin. These tribes, since the end of the last century, have, many of them, ceased to breed pure horses, and the difficulty of procuring authentic blood is now almost insurmountable. The "noble" horse-breeding tribes are few and inaccessible, and in cases where valuable animals sometimes leave Arabia, where every good horse is an object of interest, there is always great danger of substitution for inferior animals before they reach Europe, as it is seldom that the actual purchaser is the importer first hand.

A Society here has recently claimed several unspecified "types" for the pure Arab. This is entirely mistaken, and the whole question both of type and history will be dealt with conclusively in the late Lady Anne Blunt's book, shortly to be published by Lady Wentworth. The study of the nomad Beduins and the Arabian horse was Lady Anne Blunt's life's work, and learned eastern professors and students of Arabic literature consulted her for many years on difficult interpretations of ancient writers, the head of the Azhar university accepting her decisions as final. For 45 years she lived in intimate converse with members of the best horse-breeding

RAZAZ

RESM

AZREK

RIJM

MAREUK

DAOUD

## STALLIONS.

Ancestors of the Crabbet Stud.

tribes of central Arabia. The real Arab is to the Syrians and Mesopotamians what the pure bred greyhound is to a mongrel; the differences in the Barb and the Arab are fundamental structural ones as well.

The Barb is ram headed and " goose rumped," with convex skull, a low set tail carried trailing between the hocks, the eye is small and what may be termed triangular in setting, and is placed high in a narrow skull. The true Arab is gazelle headed with an upturned profile, a high set tail gaily carried, and his eye is enormous, a blunted oval, extremely wide open and placed very low in a broad, deep and wide skull tapering sharply to a fine muzzle. His arched neck and broad level quarters and back and rounded symmetrical outlines are in direct opposition to the ewe or straight neck and narrow drooping quarters of the Syrian, whose straight profile, narrow head and jaw and smaller eye are of quite a different type. Both Barb and Syrian are high on the leg, narrow chested and angular compared to the Arabian, who should be short on the leg, with powerful hocks and legs like steel.

The Central Arabian is the only gazelle headed horse in the world, and this, together with his high tail carriage and incomparable fire and courage of disposition, stamps him as a race apart from all others. It is for this reason that the head and tail are so insisted on in the Arabian breed, being points quite as important as body conformation and soundness of limb, for they are the hall mark of authenticity, and though individual heads may be of varying merit, the main character of the type remains the same.

The famous horse Champion Rasim took 1st at Islington, 1921, in a class of 13, including all the best Arab Stallions in Great Britain. Rasim also took 1st in a riding class of 13; and Nasra was 1st at Islington in a class of 12. These were the hottest and biggest Arab classes on record, except a class of 19 in which Champion Mesaoud won nearly 30 years ago, and all the winners, except two third prizes, came from the Crabbet Stud.

Nasik is the grandest type of the larger size horse, being 15.1 h., with 8in. of bone.

Enormous offers have been refused for all these stallions.

ARABIAN MARE JUMPING.

IBN YASHMAK.

Champion Skowronek and Champion Rasim are supreme champions of Great Britain.

All Crabbet horses are registered in WEATHERBY'S GENERAL STUD BOOK. No Arab stud book in England is recognised by Lady Wentworth owing to horses of unknown pedigree and doubtful origin having been admitted for registration, and neither type nor the value of caste being generally understood.

The Crabbet Arabian Stud is the only Arabian Stud in the world, the whole of whose stock is eligible for registration on its own credentials and classed in the General Stud Book on a level with the thoroughbred racehorse, and which has also provided winners on the English turf. Two races of 310 miles open to all breeds were won by pure Crabbet horses of the highest Arab strains, and the three others of 300 and 260 miles in England by a pure Crabbet mare and a horse of mixed Crabbet blood competing against Arabs only.

The Crabbet Arabian Stud has sent champions and prize winners to all parts of the world, including a champion and grand champion of Australia and Egypt, and winners and leading government stallions in India, America, the Argentine, Japan, Peru, South America, Spain, Russia, Poland, New South Wales, East Africa, New Zealand, South Africa, France, Italy, Portugal, and Spain.

They have done well under all conditions and in all climates, and Crabbet is recognised as the Arabian blood to which other leading studs owe their best stock, notably Senor Ayerza's Argentine Stud, nine of whose mares and several stallions are Crabbet bred; the best Studs in Egypt, which bought 23 stallions and a filly from Crabbet in 1920, and some 30 horses from Lady Anne Blunt's Sheykh Obeyd Stud in 1918; the Indian Government Stud at Achmednagar, 33 out of whose 55 mares are by a Crabbet stallion; Mr. Brown's Maynesborough American Stud, which is almost entirely bought from Crabbet or bred from Crabbet stock, and which owes two 310 mile race winners to Crabbet, each winner having carried respectively 14½ and 17½ stone, and whose best leading stallions are from Crabbet. In 1921 63 out of 66 horses were wholly or partly Crabbet bred, and in 1924 the proportion was still 40 out of 43. The American races were won against Thoroughbreds, Morgans and other breeds.

CHAMPION PHAROAH.

CHAMPION ROSEMARY.

CHAMPION BERK.                              *Photo: Rouch.*

RIM.   (Age 2 Years).                       *Photo: Rouch.*

## *SOME RACING RECORDS.*

Some of the racing records of Crabbet-bred Arabs are as follows, and can be substantiated with names and dates:

154 miles—weight carried 11½ stone—in 30 hours 40 minutes
Twice in the same time with different horses.

| | | | | |
|---|---|---|---|---|
| 162 miles | —weight | 12st. 4lb. | —in | 17 hours. |
| 306 | „ „ | 12st. 4lb. | „ | 53h. 58m. |
| 300 | „ „ | 17½st. | „ | 52h. 33m. |
| 100 | „ „ | 17½st. | „ | 53h. 56m. |
| 310 | „ „ | 17½st. | „ | 49h. 4m. |
| 306 | „ „ | 14½st. | „ | 52h. 37m. |
| 306 | „ „ | 14½st. | „ | 51h. 26m. |
| 260 | „ „ | 17½st. | „ | 51h. |
| 300 | „ „ | 17½st. | „ | 59h. 23m. |
| 250 | „ „ | 13½st. | „ | 32h. 20m. |
| 50 | „ „ | 13½st. | „ | 4h. 15½m. |
| 60 | „ „ | 13½st. | „ | 5h. 22m. |
| *61⅘ | „ „ | 17½st. | „ | 8h. 7m. |
| *61⅘ | „ „ | 17½st. | „ | 8h. 19m. |
| *61⅘ | „ „ | 17½st. | „ | 8h. 19m. |

*These last three were done on the three final days of a 310-mile run, the distance covered each day being limited to about 60 miles. Other flat races and steeplechases have been won in England by horses bred from the Crabbet mares Basilisk, Debora, and Purple Iris.

**RANGOON.** (Age 2 Years).

**BELKA.** Owner (Mr. H. V. CLARK) up.

This famous mare, bred at Crabbet, from Rijm ex Bereyda, won the British 300 mile endurance race in 1921 by 1 hour 40 minutes, carrying 13½ stone. In 1923, she won the mile race for Arabs at Bideford, by 20 lengths, from Shahzada and others. Mr. Clark refused 5,000 guineas publicly offered for her in 1920 by Mr. Hough, after coming in among the first three in the 300 mile race of that year.

**RAMLA.** (Now the property of Mr. A. Harris, U.S.A.)

This wonderful mare, bred at Crabbet from Astraled ex Ridaa, won the Cup of America, carrying 14½ stone in a 310 mile race open to all breeds in 1919.

BASILISK (Granddam of Alfragan, Winner of the Dee Stakes).
Fifty Years Ago.

SHAHWAN.                    *Own Copyright.*
Thirty Years Ago.

CHAMPION SKOWRONEK.
Present Day Type.

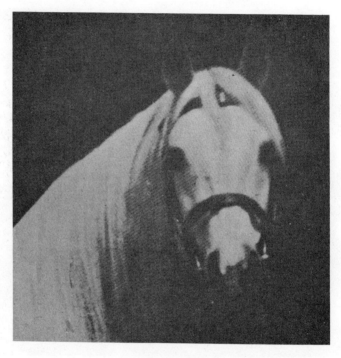

*A Typical Head.*

# *Mares.*

*Brood Mares and Fillies, the produce of Mares originally imported from Arabia. All those marked * were bred by Ali Pasha Sherif from stock imported from Arabia by Abbas I., Viceroy of Egypt.*

*Kehilan Ajuz is the generic term indicating thoroughbred from which all Strains are offshoots. Feminine is Kehilet and Kehileh.*

### Kehilan Ajuz of the Dajani Strain.

1. **CHAMPION NASRA,** Bay.  Dam Nefisa by Hadban, a Bay Hadban Enzeyhi of the Oteybeh tribe, purchased from Jakeen Ibn Aghil Sheykh of the Daajini tribe of Oteybeh and taken to Bombay in 1883 by Sheykh Ali Ibn Amr of Bussora, from whom he was purchased by Lady Anne Blunt the same year.  Hadban exported to Australia 1885.  Nefisa's Dam Dajania by a Kehilan Nowak ex a Kehileh Dajanieh from the Sebaa Anazeh.  Sire Daoud, a Dahman Nejib by Champion Mesaoud* ex Bint Nura II* by Aziz ex Bint Nura by Zobeyni ex Nura.  Mesaoud by Aziz ex Yemameh, a Grey Seglawieh Jedranieh of the rare strain of Ibn Sudan now extinct in the desert. It was bought up in Arabia by Abbas I., Viceroy of Egypt, at fabulous prices and descended to his successor, Ali Pasha Sherif, and all the best were purchased by the Crabbet Stud when the Cairo Stud was broken up.  Aziz by Harkan (Zobeyni—Harka) ex Aziza (Samhan—Bint Faras Nakadan).  Bint Nura, 2nd Prize, Crystal Palace, 1898.  Mesaoud, 1st Prize, Crystal Palace, 1896, 1897, 1898.  Nasra, 1st and Champion, Islington, 1921; 1st and Champion Gold Medal, Royal Show, 1921; 1st and Champion, Islington, 1922; 1st and Champion, Royal Show, 1922 Dam of the Champion foal Nasira and the Champion three-year-old Nisreen and the Champion colt Naseem, also of Nadra, 1st Prize, East Africa, 1923.

LADY WENTWORTH WITH ARABIAN MARES.

Photo: *Special Press.*

HAZZAM

CH. RISALA

SOMRA

NISREEN

NASIK

NAFIA

*Photo: Sport and General.*

CHAMPION NASRA and Her Colt NASEEM.

2. **NISREEN,** Bay, bred 1919. Dam Champion Nasra (No. 1). Sire Champion Nureddin, a Kehilan Ajuz of the Dajani strain by Rijm ex Narghileh by Champion Mesaoud (see No. 1) ex Nefisa (see No. 1). Rijm by Mahruss II.* whose dam was a Dahmeh Nejiba, whose sire was Mahruss I.*, a Grey Wadnan Hursan by Wazir ex Bint Saouda ex Faras Saouda of Bender Ibn Saadun. Wazir a celebrated racehorse by Zobeyni ex a Seglawieh Sudanieh. Rijm's Dam Rose of Sharon by Hadban (see No. 1) ex Rodania (see No. 9). Nisreen 2nd, Islington, 1921; Junior Champion, Islington 1922.

3. **NASHISHA,** Bay, bred 1920. Sire Champion Rasim (No. 3 Stallions). Dam Champion Nasra (No. 1). Reserve Champion, Islington, 1923.

PAIR OF ARABIAN MARES.

*Daily Sketch.*

CRABBET STALLIONS AT RICHMOND SHOW, 1924,
where the Stud won Champion Gold Medal, First, Second, Third. Reserve and V.H.C. in a strong class of fourteen entries.

BUKRA.

4. **NASIRA,** Dark Bay, bred 1921. Dam Nasra. Sire Champion Nadir by Champion Mesaoud (see No. 1), ex Nefisa (see No. 1). Nadir Champion Polo Pony Sires, Tunbridge Wells, 1913: Champion, Islington, 1911, 1913, and 1915. Nasira won the Champion Gold Medal, colt or filly, at the Royal Show, 1921, at the age of two months. Nadir is own brother to the famous stallion Mareukh (registered Narenk) who is the sire of all the best stock at the great Indian Stud at Ahmednagar.

5. **NESSIMA,** Bay. Dam Narghileh by Champion Mesaoud ex Nefisa (see both No. 1). Sire Rijm (see No. 2). Nessima 2nd Prize, Royal Show, 1920: 2nd, London, 1923. Full sister to Champion Nureddin, and half sister to Belka.

6. **NASIRIEH,** Grey, bred 1923. Dam Nisreen (No. 2). Sire Champion Skowronek.

7. **NASIFA,** Grey Filly, bred 1924. Sire Champion Skowronek. Dam Nasra (No. 1).

8. **NADIYA,** Bay Filly, bred 1924. Sire Champion Rasim. Dam Nashisha (No. 3).

## Kehilan Ajuz of the Ibn Rodan Strain.

9. **CHAMPION RISALA,** Chestnut, height 15.1. Sire Champion Mesaoud (see No. 1). Dam Ridaa by Merzuk*, a Kehilan Jellabi by Wazir (see No. 2), ex a Kehileh Jellabieh of the strain of Ibn Khalifeh Sheykh of Bahreyn. Dam of Ridaa Rose of Sharon by Hadban (see No. 1) ex Rodania, imported, bred by Ibn Rodan of the Roala tribe and taken in war from Sotamm Ibn Shaalan Sheykh of the Roala in 1880 by Tais Ibn Sharban of the Gomussa tribe of Sebaa Anazeh from whom she was purchased by the Crabbet Stud. 2nd Prize in saddle Aldershot, 1922; Champion, Islington, 1923.

*Photo: Special Press.*

**LADY WENTWORTH WITH TWO ARABIAN MARES (24 and 25 Years Old).**

10. **RISH,** Bay, 15 hands. Sire Nejran by Azrek (a Seglawi Jedran of Ibn ed Derri celebrated as a sire and for speed) ex Nefisa (see No. 1). Dam Rabla by Champion Mesaoud (see No. 1) ex Champion Rosemary by Jeroboam by Pharoah ex Jerboa, a Managhieh Hedrujieh bred at Deyr on the Euphrates her Dam from the Obeyd tribe. Her Sire a Managhi Ibn Sbeyel. Pharoah a Seglawi Jedran of Ibn ed Derri. 1st Prize Islington, 1881. Later sold to Count Potocki (see No. I Stallions). Dam of Rosemary Rodania (see No. 9).

MARES AT GRASS.

11. **RIYALA,** Dark Chestnut. A celebrated mare (sister to Ramla, sold to America and winner of the American 310 mile race open to all breeds, 1919, carrying $15\frac{1}{2}$ stone, and followed by a sprinting race). Sire Astraled by Champion Mesaoud (see No. 1) ex Queen of Sheba, an imported Bay Abeyeh Sherrakieh bred by Erheyen Ibn Alian of the Gomussa tribe of Sebaa Anazeh Dam an Abeyeh Sherrakieh. Sire a Managhi Hedruj of Ibn Gufeyfi of the Gomussa tribe. She was sold by her breeder on shares in 1877 to Beteyen Ibn Mirshid, Supreme Sheykh of the Gomussa, and purchased from him in 1878. Dam Ridaa (see No. 9). Riyala 2nd and R. Champion, Islington, 1922, Nasra being 1st.

12. **RIM,** Dark Chestnut. Sister to No. 11. Dam of Raswan, the Reserve Champion Foal, Royal Show, 1921.

13. **RISSLA,** Chestnut, bred 1917. Sire Champion Berk by Seyal (Mesaoud—Sobha) ex Bukra (Ahmar—Bozra, see No. 4 Stallions). Dam Champion Risala (No. 9). Sobha by Wazir (see No. 2) ex Selma I. the Hamdanieh Simrieh of Abbas Pasha. Berk won 1st at Islington, 1909, 1910, and 1911. Ahmar (1st Prize London, 1898) by Azrek ex Queen of Sheba (see No. 11). Rissla R. Champion, Royal Show, 1922. She is remarkable for her extremely brilliant action.

14. **RAFINA,** Chestnut, bred 1919. Sire Rustem. Dam Risala (No. 9). Rustem full brother to Nos. 11 and 12.

15. **RIFLA,** Chestnut, bred 1920. Sire Champion Rasim (No. 3 Stallions). Dam Rim (No. 12).

15A. **ROSSANA,** Grey, bred 1921. Sire Champion Skowronek (No. 1 Stallions). Dam Rose of Hind by Rejeb (Champion Mesaoud see No. 1—Champion Rosemary see No. 10) ex Rose Diamond by Azrek (see No. 10) ex Rodania (see No. 9).

RIYALA.      *Photo: Sport and General.*

16. **RIFALA,** Grey, bred 1922. Sire Champion Skowronek (No. 1 Stallions). Dam Rissla (No. 13). Rifala 1st Prize and R. Champion, Horsham Show, 1923: 2nd R. Champion, Royal Show, 1922.

17. **RISHNA,** Chestnut, bred 1923. Sire Champion Nureddin (No. 6 Stallions). Dam Rish (No. 10).

18. **RIMINI,** Grey, bred 1923. Sire Champion Skowronek (No. 1). Dam Rim (No. 12).

19. **RAYYA,** Brown. Sire Rustem, full brother to No. 11. Dam Riada by Champion Mesaoud ex Champion Rosemary (see No. 10).

20. **RISHAFA,** Chestnut Filly, bred 1924. Sire Champion Nureddin. Dam Rish (No. 10).

21. **RAMAYANA,** Chestnut Filly, bred 1924. Sire Champion Nureddin. Dam Riyala (No. 11).

## Seglawi Jedran of Ibn ed Derri.

22. **CHAMPION MARHABA,** Bay. Sire Daoud (see No. 1). Dam Mabruka by Azrek (see No. 10) ex Meshura imported, bred by Sheykh Berghi Ibn ed Derri of the Resallin related to the Gomussa tribe of Sabaa Anazeh. Sire a Managhi Hedruj of Ibn Sbeyel from Dervish Ibn Maas of the Moaheeb of the Gomussa. Dam Berghi's bay mare wounded and died after Sotamm Ibn Shaalan's raid. Her Sire a Seglawi Mureyfi Obeyri of Obeyd el Belaas of the Roala. Her Dam the chestnut mare of Simdan of the Gomussa from the Roala (bought eventually by Abbas Pasha) whose dam was the chestnut Seglawieh Jedranieh mare of Daghir and whose sire a Seglawi Jedran of Aaatta el Agdaa of the Ferjeh. Champion at Horsham Show, 1923. Half sister to Champion Nasra.

23. **BATTLA,** Grey. Sire Razaz by Astraled (see No. 11) ex Rose of Hind (see No. 15A). Dam Bukra (see No. 4 Stallions).

23A. **BAHREYN,** Grey, bred 1924. Sire Rizyan by Ibn Yashmak (see No. 24) ex Rijma by Rijm ex Champion Risala (No. 9).

AJJAM.　　Photo: Special Press.

## Abeyan Sherrak.

24. **AJJAM;** Chestnut, bred 1915. Sire Ibn Yashmak by
    Feysul* by Ibn Nura ex el Argaa ex Bint Jellabiet
    Feysul. Ibn Nura by Sotamm I. (by Sueyd, a Seglawi
    Jedran of Ibn Sudan ex the Dahmeh Nejiba of Khalil
    el Hajry) ex Bint Nura II. by Aziz (see No. 1) ex Bint
    Nura I. (Zobeyni—Nura, a Dahmeh Nejiba). Dam of
    Ibn Yashmak, Yashmak (Shahwan—Yemama II., a
    Kehileh Jellabieh of Abbas Pasha). Shahwan by
    Wazir (see No. 2) ex a Dahmeh Shahwanieh great
    granddaughter of the mare of Ibn Khalifeh. Dam
    Ajramieh by Mesaoud (see No. 1) ex Asfura by Azrek
    (see No. 10) ex Queen of Sheba (see No. 11).

## Hamdani Simri.

25. **SOMRA,** White. Sire Daoud (see No. 1). Dam Siwa by
    Ahmar (see No. 4 Stallions) ex Sobha by Wazir (see
    No. 2) ex Selma I. the Hamdanieh Simrieh of Abbas
    Pasha. Silver Medal, Horsham Show, 1923. Somra is
    half sister to Champion Nasra.

26. **SELIMA,** Brown. Sire Astraled (see No. 11). Dam Selma
    II. by Ahmar (see No. 4 Stallions) ex Sobha by Wazir
    (see No. 2), 2nd Prize, Ranelagh, 1922, and Horsham,
    1923.

27. **SHELIFA,** Grey, bred 1922. Sire Champion Skowronek (No. 1 Stallions). Dam Selima (No. 26).

28. **SARDHANA,** Bay Filly, bred 1924. Sire Champion Nureddin. Dam Selima (No. 26).

*Photo: Special Press.*

## Managhi Ibn Sbeyel.

29. **FERDA,** Bay. Sire Rustem (full brother to No. 11). Dam Feluka by Champion Mesaoud ex Ferida, imported by Lady Anne Blunt from the Shammar tribe. Feluka 2nd Prize, London, 1920: 3rd Royal, 1920: 2nd London, 1921. Ferda 3rd Prize, Ranelagh, 1922; 3rd Prize, Horsham, 1923.

30. **FEJR,** Dark Chestnut, bred 1911. Sire Rijm (see No. 2 Mares). Dam Feluka (see No. 29 Mares).

31. **FANTANA,** Chestnut, bred 1922. Sire Nasik. Dam Ferda (No. 29).

32. **FASILA,** Dark Chestnut, bred 1923. Sire Champion Rasim. Dam Fejr (No. 30).

HADBAN.

RASEEM.    (Age 2 Years).

# *STALLIONS*

*Photo: Special Press.*

CHAMPION SKOWRONEK.
Lady Wentworth up.

AHMAR.

# *Stallions.*

1. **CHAMPION SKOWRONEK,** a White Kehilan Ajuz of the strain imported to Poland by the Antoniny Stud. G.S.B. Vol. 24. P.P.S.B. 664. Hurlingham 12003, and R.S.B. Sire Ibraham (white) by Heijer -ex Lafitte. Dam Yaskoulka, 99 vii, R.S.B., a Kehilet Ajuz by Rymnik ex Epopea by Dervish ex Lyra, 198 R.S.B. Count Joseph Potocki's famous Arab Stud at Antoniny dated from before the year 1700. It was destroyed by the Bolsheviks during the Great War, 1916. Skowronek Reserve Champion to Rasim, Islington, 1921; 1st and Champion, London, 1922; 1st and Champion, Royal Show, 1922; 1st and Champion, Horsham Show, 1923; 1st, Chester Show, 1923. Skowronek is the sire of the foal which won the Ranelagh Cup, 1922, and of the Reserve for Gold Medal Foal, Royal Show, 1921; sold for a record price; and of the Champion and Reserve Champion Foals, Royal Show, 1922; and of the 1st and 2nd prize winners Horsham Show, 1923. This horse is the ideal type which Abbas Pasha I., Viceroy of Egypt, spent a fortune in collecting from the desert where it is now unprocurable. No more perfect specimen has ever been imported to England. The pure white colour is very rare and greatly valued. Lady Anne Blunt spent the last twenty years of her life in a vain search for a horse of Skowronek's type. 1st and Gold Champion Medal, Richmond, 1924, in a class of 14 entries.

*Daily Mirror.*

CHAMPION SKOWRONEK.

2. **MANYANA,** a Chestnut (Seglawi Jedran of Ibn ed Derri),
bred 1924.   Sire Rafeef.   Dam Champion Marhaba
(No. 22).

RAFEEF.

*Press Photo Agency.*
CHAMPION RASIM.

3. **CHAMPION RASIM,** a Golden Chestnut Kehilan Ajuz of
Ibn Rodan. Sire Feysul* by Ibn Nura* ex El Argaa
ex Bint Jellabiet Feysul. Ibn Nura by Sottam I., by
Sueyd ex the Dahmeh Nejiba of Khalil el Hajry.
Dam of Ibn Nura, Bint Nura II. (see No. 1). The
Jellabiet Feysul was purchased by Abbas I. from
Feysul Ibn Turki Emir of Riad, who had her from
Ibn Khalifeh Sheykh of Bahreyn, possessor of that
strain through the Ajman tribe of Eastern Nejd.
Dam of Rasim, Champion Risala (No. 9 Mares).
Rasim Champion at Islington, 1921, and 1st in Riding
Class; Champion Gold Medal, Royal Show, 1921;
Champion Gold Medal, Ranelagh, 1921; 1st Riding
Class, Islington, 1922; 1st Riding Class, Aldershot,
1922; Sire of H.M. the King's Winning Horse,
Islington, 1922; 1st and Champion, London, 1923;
1st Rusper, 1923; 2nd to Skowronek, Richmond, 1924.

NASEEM.

4. **HAZZAM,** a Seglawi Jedran of Ibn Sudan  Bay.  Sire
Champion Berk by Seyal by Champion Mesaoud (see
No. 1 Mares) ex Sobha by Wazir (see No. 2 Mares).
Dam Hilmyeh by Ahmar (by Azrek, see No. 10 Mares,
ex Queen of Sheba, see No. 11 Mares) ex Bint Helwa*
by Aziz* (see No. 1 Mares) ex Helwa by Shueyman
(Jerboa—Shueyma) ex Horra by Zobeyni ex Ghazieh.
Dam of Berk, Bukra by Ahmar (Azrek—Queen of
Sheba) ex Bozra by Pharaoh (see No. 10 Mares) ex
Basilisk. Basilisk a Seglawieh Jedranieh of Ibn ed
Derri, granddam of Alfragan, winner of the Dee
Stakes. Bozra, a winner. Hazzam has racing blood
on both sides, through Basilisk and Wazir.  Berk,
Ahmar, and Azrek were all famous for their brilliant
action.  Ahmar, 1st Islington; Champion Berk, 1st
Islington, 1909, 1910, and 1911.

5. **NASIK,** a Golden Bay, Kehilan Dajani, 15.1 h.  Sire Rijm
(see No. 2 Mares).  Dam Narghileh by Champion
Mesaoud ex Nefisa (see both No. 1 Mares).  Nasik is
a magnificent horse of the type best liked by the
Bedouins, having style and quality in a superlative
degree.

6. **CHAMPION NUREDDIN,** a Dark Chestnut, full brother to No. 5. This is the tallest authentic pure Arab on record, being nearly 16 hands, and strong in proportion without loss of style. Winner of the Champion Cup, Ranelagh, 1919; 1st at the Royal Show, 1919; and Cup at Ranelagh, 1922. Both 5 and 6 are by the same sire as " Crabbet," sold to America and winner of the 310 mile race, 1921, competing against Thoroughbreds and carrying 17½ stone. Also half brother to Belka, bred at Crabbet and winner of the English 300 mile race, 1921, carrying 13½ stone. Belka also won by 20 lengths on a tight rein the Arab race of one mile in 1923, beating Shahzada, the winner of two big races, at even weights, carrying 10 stone. Five thousand guineas has been refused for Nureddin to go to the East, and 5,000 guineas was publicly offered by Mr. Hough and refused by Mr. Clark for Belka. He sired the Junior Champion, London, 1922; and the 1st, 2nd, and 3rd Prize Winners, 1921.

NASIK.

*Photo: Sport and General.*

**NAUFAL.**
(Winner of First and Challenge Cup, Dublin, 1924.)
Recently sold to Ireland.

MIRAGE.

CHAMPION NUREDDIN.

7. **RAFEEF,** a Golden Chestnut Kehilan Rodan. bred 1917.
Sire Nasik (No. 5). Dam Riyala (No. 11). R. Champion, Royal Show, 1922; also 2nd and Cup, Ranelagh, 1922; 2nd, Chester, 1922; 3rd to Champion Skowronek and Champion Rasim, Richmond, 1924.

8. **NAFIA.** a Chestnut Kehilan Dajani, bred 1916. 15 h. Sire Ibn Yashmak (see No. 24 Mares). Dam Nessima (No. 5).

9. **RASWAN,** Grey Kehilan Rodan, bred 1921. Sire Champion Skowronek. Dam Rim (No. 12 Mares). Raswan 2nd and Reserve for Championship Medal, Royal Show, 1921, at the age of 2 months; 2nd Prize, London, 1923; 2nd Prize and R. Champion, Horsham, 1923.

10. **RANGOON,** a Grey Kehilan Rodan, bred 1921. Sire Skowronek. Dam Rish (No. 10 Mares).

11. **NASEEM,** a Grey Kehilan Dajani, bred 1922. Sire Champion Skowronek. Dam Champion Nasra (No. 1). Gold Medal, Royal Show, 1922.

12. **FARRASH,** a Bay Managhi Ibn Sbeyel, bred 1923. Sire Champion Nadir (see No. 4 Mares). Dam Ferda (No. 29).

13. **RASEEM,** a Chestnut Kehilan Rodan, bred 1922. Sire Champion Rasim. Dam Rim (No. 12 Mares). 3rd Prize Horsham Show, 1923.

14. **SHEFIK,** a Bay Hamdani Simri, bred 1922. Sire Champion Nadir (see No. 4 Mares). Dam Safarjal by Champion Berk (see No. 13 Mares) ex Somra (No. 25 Mares).

15. **A BROWN** Kehilan Rodan, bred 1924. Sire Champion Naufal. Dam Rafina, by Rustem (see No. 19 Mares) ex Risala (No. 9). Naufal by Sotamm II. by Astraled (see No. 11 Mares) ex Selma (see No. 25). Dam of Naufal Narghileh (see No. 5).

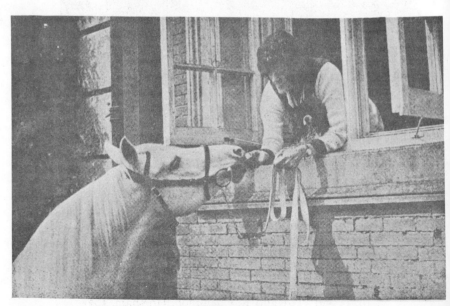

"GOOD MORNING."           *Photo: Special Press*

RIFALA.

RISSAL.

NASIRIEH.

Yearlings by Champion Skowronek.

A TWO YEAR OLD COLT.

HAZZAM.

16. **SHAREER,** a Bay Hamdani Simri, bred 1923. Sire Champion Nureddin (No. 6). Dam Selima (No. 26).

17. **NISSAR,** a Bay Kehilan Dajani, bred 1923. Sire Champion Nadir (see No. 4 Mares). Dam Champion Nasra (No. 1 Mares).

18. **RASEYN,** a Dark Grey Kehilan Rodan, bred 1923. Sire Champion Skowronek (No. 1). Dam Rayya (No. 19 Mares).

19. **RISSAL,** a Grey Kehilan Rodan, bred 1923. Sire Champion Skowronek. Dam Rissla (No. 13).

CHAMPION RASIM.                    *Central News*

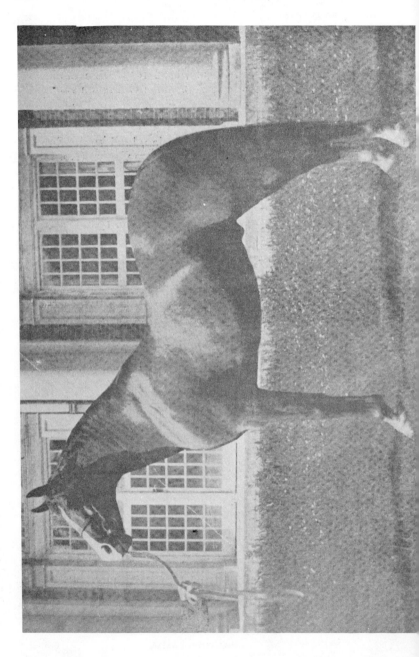

Photo: *Sport and General.*

**NASIK.**

20. **ASTRALIS,** a Chestnut Abeyan Sherrak, bred 1923. Sire Champion Rasim (No. 3). Dam Ajjam (No. 24).

21. **MINARET,** a Bay Dahman Om Amr, bred 1916. Sire Zubeir by Rafyk ex Rose of Jericho by Kars (a Seglawi Jedran of Ibn Sbeyni of the Mehed tribe of Fedaan Anazeh) ex Rodania (see No. 9). Dam Abdul by Rafyk ex Dahna by Kars ex Dahma, a Dahmeh Om Amr of Ibn Hemsi of the Gomussa tribe and sold him to Oueynan Ibn Said of the Gomussa. Zubeir own brother to the Grand Champion of Australia. Champion Rafyk by Azrek (see No. 10 Mares) ex Rose of Sharon by Hadban (see No. 1 Mares) ex Rodania (see No. 9 Mares).

22. **FARIS,** a Chestnut Managhi Ibn Sbeyel, bred 1924. Sire Champion Nureddin. Dam Fejr (No. 30).

23. **INDRA,** a Bay Kehilan Dajani, bred 1924. Sire Champion Rasim. Dam Nisreen (No. 2).

24. **RAJPUTANA,** a Bay Kehilan Dajani, bred 1924. Sire Nasik. Dam Rissla (No. 13).

25. **RUFEYFAN,** a Grey Kehilan Rodan, bred 1924. Sire Champion Rasim. Dam Rifla (No. 15).

26. **RAHAL,** a Chestnut Kehilan Rodan, bred 1924. Sire Champion Nureddin. Dam Rim (No. 12).

27.\***HUSEYNI,** a Grey Kehilan Ajuz, bred 1924. Sire Champion Skowronek. Dam Hanna by Rijm ex Howa by Azrek ex Harra by Rataplan, a Dahman om Amr winner of races. Dam of Harra Harik by Kars ex Hagar imported from Arabia in 1878 by Lady Anne Blunt.

28. **FEJRAN,** a Chestnut Managhi Ibn Sbeyel, bred 1924. Sire Champion Rasim. Dam Ferda (No. 29).

NOTE.—MIRAGE. Lady Wentworth has also at Crabbet a very fine white stallion imported by King Faisal of Irak from the Denednasha tribe, to whom he paid £500 for the horse through General-Haddad Pasha, who identified the horse and his history in 1922. He is a Kehilan Ajuz of the Denednasha Nejd strain, but will not be incorporated in the Crabbet Stud until King Faisal's signature has been obtained.

MINARET.

---

*This colt was bred and presented to the Crabbet Stud by Miss Lyon.*